Farida, the Queen of Egypt

A Memoir of Love and Governance

Farouk Hashem
and Morad Abou-Sabe

authorHOUSE®

AuthorHouse™ LLC
1663 Liberty Drive
Bloomington, IN 47403
www.authorhouse.com
Phone: 1-800-839-8640

Published by AuthorHouse   08/22/2014

ISBN: 978-1-4918-7174-4 (sc)
ISBN: 978-1-4918-7173-7 (e)

Library of Congress Control Number: 2014904557

Contents

About The Book

The turns of the Egyptian history are like a continuous chain of events, sometimes plagued with horrors and misfortunes and, at times, filled with brilliant historical achievements. All together, they form unyielding pages of history that remain there with the truths for all to discover and contemplate.

This Book, "Farida, the Queen of Egypt, a memoir of Love and Governance", is the authentic love story of Safinaz Zul-Faquar, who later took the royal name Queen Farida, and the young Prince of Egypt, Farouk the First. It is the story that the late queen told in her own words, as she described the joyful times she had as a young teen falling in love with this handsome young adolescent Prince Farouk, who was about to be crowned the King of Egypt. Talking about how she was enthralled into the romance of her life, when King Farouk chose her to be his wife and the Queen of Egypt.

Queen Farida's story describes her love for Farouk and her passion for wanting to make her life at the Royal Palace, the fairytale every young girl dreams about. It also describes her struggles with the Royal Palace Court and the King's entourage of assistants and servants, who vied for controlling the palace life over her will. Farida describes how she fought the Palace corruption and how she tried to protect Farouk, who was constantly steered towards the life of lust and women and not the life of an honorable King, husband and father and a model for his people?

Farida described how it all ended, after eleven years of persistence to make it right, with no options but to demand her divorce from King

Farouk. With her divorce in 1948, hell broke loose over Farouk's incompetence and the tragedies mounted leading to his humiliation and ultimate exile to Italy, on July 26th, 1952, after the Egyptian Military Revolution.

Farida's life story continues when she turned to Art, after her divorce and losing her crown. Art became her passion and the way for her salvation after her troubled marriage and the overthrow of her husband King Farouk. She describes her long journey moving from one place to another, her financial highs and lows, when she could not meet her own living expenses. She describes how she met the three Egyptian Presidents, Nasser, Sadat and Mubarak, in search for a decent life in her homeland, Egypt, by the Nile and the Pyramids.

All in all, this book is the story of Queen Farida's life with the ups and downs that characterized her life's struggle for no fault of her own. It was just her destiny and she remembered every part of it as if they were just happening.

Translator's Preface

My first and only meeting with the late Queen Farida was in the summer of 1986, at my sister-in-law's residence in Zamalek, Cairo, Egypt. My wife Mouchira and I were visiting her sister, Mervat M. Mumtaz, in the summer of 1986. Queen Farida, the cousin of Dr. Hassan Mumtaz, Mervat's husband, was also visiting. Our meeting was a brief social meeting in which Queen Farida talked about her artworks, among other topics. Because my wife and I had been living in the United States for many years, I talked to Queen Farida about the possibility of arranging an art exhibit for her in the United States. At the time, I felt an exhibit for the queen's artwork in Princeton, New Jersey, would offer a great opportunity for her and an opening for exhibitions all over the United States.

After our meeting in Zamalek, I wanted to pursue my offer to Queen Farida, but unfortunately as time passed us by, we never had the opportunity to do that. Two years later, I learned of her passing, closing the chapter on that possibility.

In 2006, many years later, I met Ambassador Farouk Hashem in Cairo. My wife and I were invited to dinner at his home in Heliopolis. That was the start of a long relationship with the Hashem's since. During our dinner conversation, the subject of Queen Farida came up, and the idea of this translation came about. Ambassador Hashem told me about his book that he had published in Arabic years earlier about the queen. It was of great interest to both of us to have it translated into the English language for publication in the United States.

It took a great deal of effort to give this book the best presentation possible. Translating from the rich Arabic language to English was not an easy task. Although I wanted to ensure the most authentic translation I could, I quickly recognized that a literal word-for-word translation would lose all the beauty of the book and the essence of the compelling story of Queen Farida. As such, this book presents the struggles and triumphs of Queen Farida based on the Arabic narrative of my friend and colleague, Farouk Hashem.

Farida, The Queen of Egypt: Memories of Love and Governance is presented as a novel on the life of the queen; her love story with her knight in shining armor, King Farouk; and his struggles with the governance of the country, Egypt. As a witness to the events from the halls inside the royal palace and through her eleven years as the queen of Egypt (January, 1938- November 17th, 1948). Queen Farida told her story to Ambassador Farouk Hashem.

The book includes rare photographs of the queen's life inside and outside the royal palace. Copies of some of her artworks and official royal declarations are included. I have also included other documents from the Egyptian Revolutionary Council, exiling King Farouk on July 26, 1952. These documents are included as appendices.

Morad Abou-Sabe', PhD
Princeton, New Jersey

Author's Preface

This book is not a diary of the late Queen Farida, the queen of Egypt. Nor is it a book about the political history of Egypt during her tenure as the first lady of Egypt for eleven years when she lived as the devoted wife and companion for King Farouk. It is a collection of memories of the late queen that she narrated to me, where I was the quiet, attentive listener. It is a semblance of memories that were flowing from the natural ability of a storyteller. That was Farida. It was not an intended narration to me. Nor did I lure her to tell it. The friendship between us prompted her to express her story to me. It was indeed a reflection of what transpired throughout her life. I was there for her whenever we had the opportunity and clarity of mind to discuss the events she wanted to talk about.

I saw her smiling, heard her laughing, and saw her upset and angry when it was necessary. I was with her through her most difficult moments, and there were many, but at no time did I see her showing any bitterness. With her pride, she overcame pain, the kind that most—except for the rare ones—would succumb to. Her artistic spirit held her fragile body high above the tragedy that had befallen her throughout her adult life. Painting was her sanctuary and brought her comfort.

After the opening of one of her art exhibits one evening, she told me, "Art saved me from insanity."

She was proud and shy, quiet but firm, but she had softness in her voice that spelled determination and strong will. She described a great deal of the ups and downs in her lifelong journey. There she faced with strong determination the debauchery and disarray in the affairs of the royal palace. She expressed her disapproval and disgust over all that had been happening behind the closed doors of the palace. She talked about how she resisted falling to these ills with stubbornness and without any concern for her crown and the royal position she held. She would have no hesitation giving it all up, rejecting Farouk and the royal life she had come into. She eventually did when she asked for her divorce eleven years later. She had the sincerest of intentions to be the loyal queen to the king she loved and married, but not at the expense of her pride, honor, and dignity. She preferred to keep her dignity and the love of the Egyptian people despite her concerns over the kingdom and Farouk himself. She recognized that exposing the palace corruption could only be done as a living witness on the inside.

Farida remained a reservoir of the secrets of the palace, where everything was held tightly inside here until the writing of this book. These memories can only be told with confidence and honesty, as Farida herself did. It is, after all, her personal memories.

She was like a fortune-teller when she told me, "I told you a great deal about myself that no one else knows. Do you think you'll write a book about me?"

I smiled but gave no answer. I was seeing her off at the airport in Bahrain. She was going to see her daughters in Switzerland when she told me that. I had not actually thought of writing this book until that moment. As the plane flew into the skies, I answered to myself, "Why not? Why couldn't there be a book about Farida. I'll do that someday."

Here I am, writing this book. No historical format compels me, as would have been necessary were it a historical narrative. I write it without any chronology. It's a story that someone told me, the same person who was remembering, at times with great agony, the events that shaped her life and, I might add, the life of a nation at a time when she had the inside story of what was actually happening.

Farouk Hashem
Heliopolis, Cairo, Egypt

How I Met the Queen

I did not know Farida, the former queen of Egypt, before 1976, except through her pictures in the newspapers and magazines. That year, I was working as a consular at the Egyptian Embassy in London. I was participating as the Egyptian representative in the preparation for a festival for the arts and civilization of the Islamic world with all of its regions. At that time, Queen Farida was living in Paris and had specifically come to London to attend the festival. There, I was introduced to her for the first time and learned of her interest in Islamic art. After the festival was over, Queen Farida left London with a promise that we would stay in touch and continue our dialogue about art.

Islamic art occupied a great deal of Queen Farida's thoughts. It reflected her innermost beliefs. I kept my promise and made sure throughout my service in London to always be in touch with her. I also followed up on her intellectual and artistic activities in Paris and shared my own with her from London until I completed my services at the Embassy and returned to Egypt.

In 1986, ten years later, I saw Queen Farida again. My wife and I were attending a dinner party, and to our surprise, the queen was right there. There, we had the opportunity through our host and his family to have an elegant private evening at a gathering that was primarily a family dinner.

That evening, the former queen was graceful without pretense. She was simple and fragile in her own way. The evening extended well after dinner to the wee hours of the morning until dawn. Her conversation was so enlightening that we did not feel the hours passing us by. After all, she was talking among friends. She told us about her life since she was a child and about her family. She told us how Safinaz (her birth name) met King Farouk. She told us about the engagement, the royal trip and the way her marriage was consummated. She talked about how she and Farouk differed and how their differences led to her decision after eleven years of marriage to end it all and ask for her divorce. She talked about the king's sisters and the way she won their friendship, especially Princess Faiza, who had been living for years within the walls of the royal palace. She talked about Egyptian politics, the political parties of the time, and the decadent royal court that often controlled the reins of governance. She spoke about the many tragedies and events that she witnessed and lived through. All that, Farida spelled out in great detail and from a very vivid memory. I still remember how, after she was finished with one story, she would go into a deep sigh and say "Oh God" as if she were awakening from a horrible dream or pushing away the ghost of an ugly past.

I cannot forget how I felt that night, as it left me with a strong sense that the former queen had been through really hard and tragic times. As she recalled her memories, it was abundantly clear that her spirits were not well. Clearly, she had a heavy burden on her mind.

With an initiative of my own, as we were leaving, I proposed to her that we do an exhibit for her artwork in Bahrain. Deep in my heart, I felt that would help lift up her spirits, at least for a while. She agreed, but on the condition that it would not be overly burdensome to me. I assured her that it would not and I would get in touch with my friends, my college mates from the ruling family in Bahrain. Ambassador Moustafa Kamal, the *charge' daffier* of the Bahraini office in Cairo and who later became Bahrain's ambassador to Egypt. I talked to Ambassador Kamal about my idea, and he welcomed it without hesitation. He gave me some time to prepare for the queen's art exhibit in his country.

As we planned for the exhibit, it so happened that a foreign head of state visited Bahrain, and we agreed that Farida's visit and her exhibit would take place immediately at the end of that presidential visit. Ambassador Kamal suggested mid-October of the same year would be the appropriate time so the former queen would have the opportunity to meet the crown prince of Bahrain. At the time of the visit, a new ambassador, Ambassador Mohamed Al Mahmeed, had replaced his predecessor, Ambassador Kamal, in Cairo.

As disciplined and organized as Farida was, she invited me to her modest apartment in Maadi and requested I bring my secretary with me to prepare the exhibit portraits for shipping. She was keen to have the artwork get to Bahrain before we did. We spent the whole day with Farida as she prepared her art pieces. There were fifty large paintings and a comparable number of smaller ones. Farida planned to take the small paintings as accompanying baggage when she traveled to the exhibit.

While we were preparing the exhibit shipment at her house, Queen Farida talked about her passion with nature and expressed her disappointment about how Egyptian cities had become transformed into a landscape of concrete, the green color had disappeared, and the absence of open space had become a detriment to people's health. She pointed out how she made nature the focal point of her paintings. She described how she oftentimes painted the Nile and the Egyptian villages with its farmers from her memory of them. These recollections came back with fondness and reminded her of the early days of her marriage. It was there that she spent those early days in Anshas, the same place where her kingdom eventually collapsed.

We went our separate ways after she prepared the traveling exhibit to meet again in the same week with my wife at her house for high tea.

An Apartment Wrapped in Sadness and Sorrow

Queen Farida lived in a small studio apartment in a multistory building in Maadi. I hadn't closely noticed the apartment in my first visit with my secretary, as I did during our tea invitation with my wife. Before we went for our visit, Queen Farida cautioned me on the phone that my wife and I should be careful with the building elevator. It might suddenly stop between floors for no apparent reason. The power might actually go off without warning. She expressed her displeasure with the landlord because he did not give these matters any importance despite its danger to the residents. Queen Farida gave us comfort in that we could always walk up the stairs because she lived on the third floor.

The apartment foyer led to the front entrance where we saw an Arabesque wooden divider. That section of the apartment was where the queen received her guests. The remaining section of the apartment contained a small dining table next to the library and some of the queen's paintings. On another small table nearby, there was a picture of the queen with her daughters. And in the same frame, there was a picture of the queen with her husband, King Farouk. A small table lamp shined directly on the picture. In another corner of the table, there was a picture of her daughters—Princesses Ferial, Fawzyia, and Fadia—with their father, King Farouk. The whole apartment reflected her delicate and beautiful touches throughout. It was, however, an image full of sorrow and sadness.

The queen introduced us to her mother, ninety-year-old Zeinab Hanem. We shook hands with Zeinab Hanem as we came in the apartment. Queen Farida prepared the tea and some dessert for us by herself, and we sat down to talk. She knew I had two daughters.

However, commenting on the social behaviors of the society, she was sad as she commented, "Girls these days do not care about knowledge and learning. Girls are concentrating too much on their outward appearances, as if they were objects without substance."

The queen was sorry that Egyptians did not appreciate their heritage and historical value.

"While Egypt has the world's largest museums within its borders, the new generations of Egyptians do not have a sense of belonging to their country. Creating that sense of belonging amongst the new generations starts when boys and girls begin to learn their Egyptian history, study its antiquities, and visit its museums. To develop that sense, we should start by making admission to these museums free of charge for all Egyptians."

The queen elaborated that many of the noble values we had, disappeared or were forgotten. She was concerned as to how those who were considered the society elites were no longer the best of people in the society.

My wife and I left the former queen's apartment, amazed at how the events from decades earlier had made Farida's life so unhappy and sad. It was beyond our imagination that the beautiful person that we had just visited was the queen of Egypt during the days when Egypt was a country to contend with among the family of nations, toe-to-toe with England and France.

After our visit to Farida's apartment, we became like family, and she accepted many of our invitations for dinner and tea parties at our house. She only requested that we do not invite too many guests. She also insisted to know who would be there when we invited her.

After getting to know her for those twelve years, especially our close relationship over the last two, I had the feeling that Farida was not among those who could easily mingle with strangers. She was not comfortable getting too close to people she did not already know. She was clearly also careful with those whom she did not know firsthand. Perhaps it was because she suffered a lot from people whom she trusted and turned out to be not up to her expectations. It may also be because her life was a continuous series of struggles, specifically with women and girls who were chasing her husband or those he chased. There was also the conniving of her mother-in-law, Queen Mother Nazly, and Princess Shwekar, among others. The many members of the royal family as well as the corrupt royal court crowded Queen Farida's life at the royal palace. She did not escape their trickery and deceit, nor those of the palace elders. The foreigners, after the king's money, were a constant reminder of the degradation of the moral values in the palace. Farida knew, as she was the diligent bride of women's folly and men's fantasies and desires, that it was no different at the royal palace from that known all over the world. It was my fate that Farida confided her secrets of that period in Egyptian history, the events that shaped the royal life, the stories of the palace corruption, and the events and struggles of that period under Farouk's stewardship.

Throughout Farida's eleven-year reign as the queen and first lady of Egypt, she shared Egypt's rule with King Farouk. Readers of this book will find how much she suffered, even as the queen of Egypt, during that period. She expressed that almost literally when she said, "I would have preferred to live a happy life in a small hut than live the life I had in this great royal prison. I witnessed firsthand how much Egypt had been through of world events, scandals, and intrigue."

The Secrets of Love and Marriage

As Queen Farida started telling her story, she said, "Farouk chose me from amongst the most beautiful of girls." A red blush glowed on her face. "I saw Farouk after his return from England, after the death of his father [King Fouad]. May he rest in peace. I went with my mother to the palace to meet her friend, Queen Mother Nazly. There, I also met my friend Fawzyia, Farouk's sister. Fawzyia had invited me to visit them that same day. I went to the palace and found a number of other girls my age. I did not know at the time that Queen Mother Nazly and the king's sisters were prospecting for a bride for Farouk.

"In front of the swimming pool, we were laughing and playing, happy with the royal atmosphere. Suddenly, Farouk appeared, and the girls shouted, 'The king! The king!' And they—except for me—ran toward Farouk. I stood there in my place motionless. I actually moved away from where Farouk was standing. I stood by myself far away, close to my mother. Suddenly, I found Farouk leaving all the girls and coming toward where my mother was sitting. He asked her who I was. She answered, 'She is my daughter Safinaz.'

"He looked to where I was standing, saluted me with a nod, and left. That was the first time I saw Farouk, and I did not know at that moment that fate had chosen me to be Farouk's wife and I would be the queen of Egypt. At that time, I was sixteen years old. I was young, still a high school girl. I was not thinking of marriage. It did not dawn onto me at all that the subject of marriage would be at hand. That was my first encounter with love."

Safinaz Zul-Faquar skiing with Princess Fathia, King Farouk's
sister, in San Moreno, Switzerland, during the Royal Trip,
Fall 1937, before her engagement to King Farouk.

I asked Queen Farida while we were sitting quietly at the Diplomat
Hotel in Bahrain, "Did you really love King Farouk? When was this
love born?"

The queen laughed, and her face blushed in shyness. "In
Switzerland, our love, Farouk and I, was born. I was sure of my love

9

for him and felt his love and caring toward me. My love included everyone on that trip. That trip was among the most beautiful days of my life. I remained for more than four months on that trip. It was where our love was born and nurtured. No one was talking about Farouk picking me for his bride, but I felt it. I felt I was being tested and something was awaiting me at the end of that trip.

"Farouk's love began piercing my heart, and I felt the birth of that love from that first trip. I felt as if I were flying off the earth, high in the sky, soaring without wings and floating in the air. I was so happy, and I could feel my heart beating with happiness. Every day that passed brought new meaning, and every moment was a special one for me. Every word had its own depth. Farouk started giving me his attention and getting closer to me. I was living as if an angel from heaven were watching over me. In those days, Farouk was kind and caring.

Queen Farida, before her marriage to King Farouk, with
Farouk and his sisters, Princesses Fawzyia and Faiza, while
in Switzerland on their Royal trip in the Fall of 1937.

"That trip was, in reality, a test for me. While I was among the
king's sisters, Fawzyia, Faika, and Faiza, Farouk and his family
wanted to know my personality and examine my behavior in an
informal setting away from all formalities. I could feel the looks
in their eyes, almost going through me as they watched me. Every
day, we would play gymnastics, go skiing, or perform other physical
activities. A schedule was prepared for us to visit the different parts
of Switzerland to observe the culture out there. The king used to take
me with his sisters on his daily routine. We used to go for walks,
visit factories, go sightseeing around the town, and so on. We had
teachers with us to teach us Arabic, French, and English. I used to sit
for hours with King Farouk's sisters in the classroom to learn from
the teachers. On a daily basis, we would review the lessons and do
our homework. It was a great trip full of fun and joy.

"Although we were on a scheduled program prepared for our education, we were all very happy, especially Farouk. He used to give me special attention above all others and showed me kindness and noticeable care. From that moment, the feelings of love began to take hold in my young heart."

In Switzerland, the Royal Love Was Born

On board the *Victory of India*, the boat that Queen Farida later called "the Love Boat," was the love voyage for Farouk and Farida before his coronation as the king of Egypt. On February 27, 1937, Farouk left for Switzerland. And with him were his mother, Queen Mother Nazly, his sisters, and his royal entourage, which was made up of thirty-seven people. Also accompanying them were Farida's mother and the king's uncle, Hussein Sabry, and his wife.

They called it an educational trip. It was a prelude until the king became of legal age, after which he could return to be crowned and take the reins of power as the king of Egypt, succeeding his father, King Fouad.

Safinaz and her mother went on this four-month trip from February 27 to July 25. After which, they returned to Alexandria. On that trip, they first visited Switzerland. Participating in that trip were also Ahmed Hassanein, Farouk's personal assistant; Omar Fathi, his advisor; Abbas El-Kafrawy, his physician; and Hussein Hosni, his personal secretary.

Upon arrival in Switzerland, King Farouk started to take care of those around him and paid special attention to Safinaz, as they went skiing in the mornings with his sisters and danced at night at the hotel. They later went to Paris and then England. After which, they once again returned to Paris.

From this "royal love trip," as it was called, Queen Farida recalled her happy and joyous memories. As the little girl who was not even sixteen years old, she said, "During this trip, I got to know King Farouk, his character, and his habits, and I loved him dearly. That period was one of the most beautiful times of my life. Although I was so young for everything, my heart was trembling with Farouk's love. He was gracious and caring. I lived those one hundred and twenty days flying with the wings of love. I was that same little girl carrying her schoolbooks across her chest at the Notre Dame De Scion in Alexandria, but I surely had the most wonderful feelings about everything that was happening.

"I was getting ready for my exams, totally immersed in studying and tutoring. My father stayed up with me every night, encouraging me to study in his library. All of a sudden, my mother received an invitation from her friend, Queen Mother Nazly, to join her on a trip to Europe. The invitation was conditional though, namely I was to be with her to join my friend Princess Fawzyia and the rest of the princesses. I hesitated at first in accepting the invitation, as I was getting ready for my exams and studying my courses. The trip would be several months long, but somehow, I had an inner feeling that this trip would change my life. I agreed to go on that royal trip and actually convinced my father, with the help of my mother, to agree that we go with Farouk to Europe.

"Suddenly, I found myself in the middle of the king's family and his associates. I could see the special attention of the young king focused on me. I actually felt I had gotten all of his attention, and at that moment, our love was born again in San Moreno, Italy. By that time, I considered his family as my own and his court as my new extended family. The trip was amongst the best and most beautiful days of my entire life with Farouk."

In the tales of her memories from the love boat, before she was engaged to Farouk, Farida talked about the story of how Farouk had become so attached to her that he could not bear leaving her.

"One day, when I was skiing with his sisters in Switzerland I fell and sprained my ankle. They carried me screaming and crying from the severity of my pain. I was afraid that something might have happened that would prevent me from walking on my feet and missing that daily royal program. While I was screaming from my pain, I saw Farouk, while still skiing and shouting at his sisters with anger, blaming them and accusing them of being careless. He cautioned them about what would happen if they were not careful and diligent. He did not address me and directed his comments to them, saying, 'This is the last time I'll let Safinaz take part in this foolishness.' He told them in a stern and serious tone, 'I'll give my orders that Safinaz does not ski with you again.' At that moment and even though he gave orders that would limit my freedom to ski and prevent me from this fun hobby, I was happy, and his decision flattered me.

"His sisters shouted back in protest, but he did not turn to them. He went to his mother and ordered her to do exactly as he directed. He then turned toward me, asking I not ski with them in this dangerous fashion. His mother laughed and said to Farouk, blaming him, 'You can talk to your sisters all you want, but it is not your place talking to Safinaz, or for that matter to your sisters, I am here, and I am not dead yet that you control them. As for Safinaz, her mother, Zeinab Hanem, is here, and she alone has the right to give her orders.'

"Farouk answered back, 'But it matters to me, as I do not want her to fall or die, and I am sure that, if they continue this carelessness, you'll go back losing at least one of your daughters.' His mother quickly responded, 'Is that because you love Safinaz?' Farouk did not answer his mother's question, and his face blushed visibly. He took my hand, ordered a cup of tea for me, and made sure that my leg was fine. We sat together far away talking. At that moment, the queen mother was sure that Farouk had fallen in love with me and chosen me to be the queen of Egypt, his partner for life."

The former queen sighed. "Strangely, it was also my mother's feeling when she asked me every day thereafter. 'What is between you and Farouk?' I would conspicuously tell her, 'Nothing.' In reality, we were living a life full of love and happiness. It was the anxious and daring youth in us. No limits bound our dreams until our love was crowned with the engagement and the happy royal wedding that followed."

The Crowning of Love

"A few weeks after our return from the royal trip, where I was still living my dreams and the memories of our love in San Moreno, Farouk surprised us with a visit to our palace in Alexandria, asking for my hand in marriage. At that time, Farouk had been crowned as the king of Egypt, succeeding his father, the late King Fouad. I knew that love had brought us together during the winter trip, but I did not know that Farouk would come back so quickly to propose to me. I was happy, even more so, that Farouk came to propose and I would be the next queen of Egypt. My mother was even happier as my marriage to Farouk would strengthen her friendship with Queen Mother Nazly and the royal family.

"Those events were not without their anxious moments. After all, in my father's eyes, I was still a little girl. At that time, I was only sixteen years old, and Farouk was only eighteen. My father used to tell my mother that this was child's play. However, after my mother's persistence and much convincing, my father agreed to the engagement, insisting it would be for several years and marriage would be after that.

"At the same time, however, Farouk was insisting that the marriage would be completed quickly and six months were enough to prepare for the marriage proceedings. After which, the wedding would take place. He got his way and what he asked for. As always, Farouk managed to get what he wanted.

Queen Farida's House in Alexandria.

"I moved from Alexandria to Cairo on Farouk's request. We did not have a house in Cairo, as my whole life was in Alexandria and we only came to Cairo on rare occasions. The king quickly resolved that problem and chose a palace for us to live in Heliopolis, a suburb of Cairo. This palace was actually Alfred Beck Shamas' palace, one of the largest and most beautiful palaces in Cairo.

Alfred Bek Shamas's Palace in Cairo, where Farida
and her family moved before the Wedding.

The Grand entrance of Alfred Bek Shamas's Palace.

All my family moved to Cairo, including my mother, my father, and my two brothers, Said and Sherif. That was the first time for me to actually live in Cairo. We were happy for the move, and Farouk used to come to visit us frequently. We did not own the palace, and it was given back to its owner, Alfred Shamas, after our short residence there. Our stay was only a temporary one to complete the royal wedding arrangements.

"On Thursday, January 20, 1938, the wedding was performed at Al Kobba Palace. I wore a dress that was specially made in Paris from beautiful French lace. Laden with silver threads, the dress had long sleeves and a short tail made by Roth, one of the most famous bridal shops in Paris at the time. Light silver material and a fifteen-foot tail covered with light lace also complemented the wedding gown. The gown was simply stunning and beautiful.

Queen Farida Wedding Ceremony and Queen
Farida in her Wedding Gown.

The King and the Queen in their formal Wedding atire

"I was so happy, not just for myself, but more so for the fact that all of Egypt was celebrating my wedding. People everywhere were full of joy and happiness; my wedding was like a great festival for all members of the society. Bright lights and glitter covered the mosques, churches, streets, and squares. Strings of lights that made the night look like extensions of daylight filled Cairo streets and the streets in the other governorates. Even the Nile River was glowing night and day with celebrating boats and floats; a blanket of colorful lights and décor—a celebration by all the different classes of the society— dressed the hotels on its shores. It was just magnificent.

"That day, actually those days and nights, passed more like a dream as if we were living in the heavens above. The flowers, music, and serenading songs were in celebration of our wedding everywhere. The glimmer of love was in everyone's eyes, as all were full of joy and happiness for us. Decorations covered the palaces, ministries, and government buildings. Everyone full of smiles and joy went out in the streets to show their love and loyalty. I do not think there was ever a wedding with this grandeur and beauty, with the participation of people from all walks of life. Even private business buildings and individual homes were decorated with flowers and magnificent arrangements of colorful lights. To Cairo came groups of people from the governorates and surrounding localities, all coming to express their best wishes and show their love with parades of flowers from every town. People's celebrations were like fairy tales, telling of the love of the Egyptian people for their king and queen.

Thousands of Al-Azhar Students Celebrating the Royal Couple wedding.

وحدات الجيش المصرى يوم ١٤ يناير . وقبل حفلات العرس بخمسة أيام . تقسم بمين الولاء للملك .

The Army in full color, celebrate the Royal Wedding,
in Abdeen Square in front of Abdeen Palace.

"Unfortunately, Farouk did not savor the enormous public
outpouring of love and affection. He might not have understood

its importance at the time. I used to tell him after that, 'Do not disconnect yourself from the people who love you, the ones who showed you their loyalty and bannered around you when we got married. Do not follow those mischievous Italian workers and their corrupt entourage. Do not sell that great love, the love of the Egyptian people, for the cheap thrills of your corrupt servants and assistants.'

"The official celebration continued for three days and nights, where the people showed their love and loyalty and Egypt was all but one big family, united and strong. It was as if each family were celebrating its own sons' and daughters' weddings. Our joy was everyone's joy and a source of happiness to every member of the society. Even the army marched out in the streets to show its love and loyalty to its king. That day, they paraded in the streets and squares, chanting their oath of loyalty to the king and the government."

The Coronation and the Fall

"On our wedding day, Farouk was loved by all of his people and especially the armed forces. No one would have thought or imagined at that time in 1938 that the army that stood in attention at Abdeen Square with full loyalty and love to its king was the same army that came out on July 23, 1952, revolting against Farouk to send him out of the country and into exile. The king who was crowned fourteen years earlier was now being removed. Not only that, but the royal dynasty would be gone, and the monarchy system of government that Mohamed Ali Pasha established, going back more than a century (1805-1953), would be changed to a republic and his family's dynasty forever gone.

"The streets, squares, houses, balconies, hallways, and walkways all were turned into beautiful decorations, and every household in Egypt was fully immersed into a joyous wedding festival. All of Egypt lived in one great celebration. Joy so filled me that night that I cried with tears of happiness, not knowing I would cry years later with pain and sorrow for his overthrow. I did not know that night that the young man I loved and the one who was loved and coroneted king of Egypt would turn the same people against him with his irresponsibility and foolishness. Those same people would now support the revolution against him, happy for his resignation, removal from the throne, and exile out of Egypt.

"I saw the people on the day of his coronation carrying him high on a pedestal, and I saw them dropping him on the day of the revolution. I lived the two moments. I saw the people dancing with joy and happiness on Thursday, January 20, 1938. And I saw them again on the 23 of July 1952, dancing for his expulsion. What a difference between the two pictures, the coronation and the fall.

"I lived those moments over and over again and saw those events as they happened. I lived Farouk's coronation when people were celebrating his life with everyone ready and willing to sacrifice their lives and treasures for their king. I was also there when the army revolted against the British in support of the king on February 4, 1942. When the British surrounded the palace with their forces and demanded that Farouk change the cabinet and form a new government under Nahas Pasha, bringing the Wafd Party into power for their own contrived goals. While politicians were seeking their own goals, the military stood by Farouk in protest.

"I saw it when the army's loyalty to the nation was tested when the British crossed the bounds of Egyptian sovereignty and national honor. I saw it at the time when the armed forces would give their lives for Farouk and stood by him. I was there when Farouk himself saw his forces and his crown defended by his soldiers and officers. They were the source of his power. He got that power from the love of his people and his army.

"I saw Farouk troubled and depressed. I saw him living alone except for the evil company he kept. They were the devils of corruption that surrounded him. They left him to his sorrow and despair when it did not serve their purposes. It was too late by then when the same officers and army contingents, those who protected Farouk in years past, declaring their loyalty to the king and kingdom, now went out at the dawn of July 23, 1952, to remove him and stand by the people's revolution. The revolution was not a surprise to me. It was as though I had seen the unknown. I predicted the revolution before it happened. I actually told Farouk about my feelings only for him to reject me out of hand and tell me that I was out of my mind.

"The wedding celebrations continued for more than three days. The first day was for officiating the wedding. My father acted as my proxy in the marriage, and Sheikh Moustafa Al Maraghy, the supreme imam; Sheikh Al Azhar, the head of the Al Azhar Institution; and Sheikh Al Geddawy, the head of Egypt's Religious Court, performed the religious ceremony. In the ceremony, my Uncle Said Zul-Faquar and Ali Maher Pasha served as my two witnesses for my marriage, as the Islamic wedding certification process required.

"The Kobba Palace, where we lived, was like a glittering jewel brilliant with the lights and colors that surrounded it. People lined the streets and squares all the way from Heliopolis, where I used to live, to the Kobba Palace, where we moved after the wedding. Music was everywhere, and people were dancing on every street corner."

Al Henna, the Bridal Bachelorette Party

"On the eve of my wedding, January 19, 1938, a folkloric music group came to Heliopolis and performed in front of the palace where I was staying that night. I later learned that this was a common Egyptian tradition called Leilt El Henna. This celebration is considered the Egyptian bachelorette party where music, songs, poetry, equestrian shows, and many different types of festivities are conducted in celebration of the wedding. With all the noise and the huge crowd that gathered around the palace to watch and participate, I enjoyed the celebration, music, and equestrian dances. That night, the horses were real Arabian horses.

"Lights inside and out decorated the palace. It was like a dream palace with all the strings and cords of lights hanging on the palace walls outside and the chandeliers inside. This magnificent lighting parade made the night skies look nothing less than a sunny day. And I cannot forget the neighbors decorating their homes and palaces with décor and lights that made the whole neighborhood like paradise.

"The celebrations, fun, and beauty everywhere continued, and the people shared our joy and love. Special commemorative postage stamps and coins were issued in honor of the royal wedding as mementos that people kept. Our wedding was full of beautiful events that I still remember, as if it was yesterday. The closeness and love I had for the people were instilled in me from that first night, the eve of my wedding. I loved the Egyptian people, lived their lives, shared their dreams and aspirations, and felt their pain. I was always, in heart and soul, with the simple peasants and the labor workers, as my art and paintings later showed.

"I began to fashion my life story with Farouk as the queen of Egypt and its first lady. I did not know at the time that there would be a sad ending to it, one that would come to pass over this beautiful story that began with love and ended in divorce."

Anshas, the Love Corner, Our Love Play Site

One evening, we were having dinner at my house in Heliopolis with Queen Farida. With us were also Ambassador Mohamed Al Mahmeed, the Bahraini ambassador, and his wife. My wife Nadia and our two daughters, Amira and Ronda, accompanied us as well. As we sat down having dinner, I asked Queen Farida with obvious curiosity about her best memories with Farouk.

The queen quietly answered, "My best memories lie in my paintings, but nobody knows that secret."

I quickly responded, "But I know your paintings. They are all about the countryside, happiness, farming, and the Egyptian village. How does that relate to your memories with Farouk?"

Queen Farida leaned back and said, "The Egyptian countryside has a long history with me. It is a story deeply connected to my soul. When I recall these memories, I relive the best moments of my life, which is an enigma no one knows about. But I'll tell you my secret today." The queen was quiet for a moment. "It was right after my wedding to Farouk. We lived our wedding celebration days, travelling between Kobba and Abdeen Palace. These celebrations went on for three days.

"The first day was at Kobba Palace. That night, Thursday night, January 20, was our wedding gala night. The whole royal family, my family, nobilities of the society, heads of the ministries, many ambassadors from the diplomatic corps representing their countries, and the leading government dignitaries attended. The music was playing in every corner of the palace. The officers and soldiers were brilliant in their beautiful blue uniforms. The men and women were in their grand gala attires. Celebrities of the arts sang their best songs and melodies. Um Kulthum and Abdel Wahab serenaded with their most beautiful music and songs.

"The flowers and trees, all in beautiful and magical arrangements, made the occasion so wonderful. It was like a beautiful dream. Farouk was so tender and loving. Everyone was full of joy and happiness. It was a special night, one evening in a lifetime that could not be imagined except in fairy tales. Happiness had overcome the whole palace with everyone in it. I was full of joy, having not experienced as

29

yet the trickery of the king's entourage and the deceit of governance. One minute, I was a bride on my wedding night. The next, I was the queen of Egypt. You cannot imagine the joy of a bride on her wedding night sitting side by side with her prince and husband, the king of Egypt. It was simply unimaginable joy. Farouk and I lived for four days in total ecstasy, sharing the joy of the people. With us were the royal family and a parade of well-wishers coming from all over Egypt, far and wide. Everyone came to wish us great joy while sharing their own happiness with us.

"After these historic celebrations and after the Egyptian people at all levels expressed their joy and happiness for the occasion, Farouk whisked me to the grand terrace of the Abdeen Palace and whispered in my ear, 'I'll take you and elope to a faraway place, away from all these demonstrations and people's eyes.' I quietly asked, 'To where?' He said, 'We are going to elope to a beautiful place, Anshas, where the royal love cove is. Brilliant with its quiet beauty, greenery and water . . . ' He laughed. 'And of course your beautiful face. I did not marry all these people. I married you, and I want you alone!'

"On the evening of Monday, January 24, we left Cairo with all of its continuing celebrations, its crowds, and all the noise and went to Anshas, or as Farouk called it, the royal love cove. On the way there, I imagined the place to be a small villa or country house. Upon our arrival to Anshas, I found a grand palace surrounded with beautiful trees, flowers, and roses with beautiful green landscape as far as the eye could see. I was happy to see the first letters of our names, FF, inscribed in big letters on the huge iron gate of this great country palace surrounded by rare plants, calm, and serenity. It was just a magnificent place. I felt at that time that this was paradise. Truly this palace was like heaven on earth for me. Farouk and I spent fourteen days in this paradise that was Anshas. They were the best days of our lives, the whole eleven years of our marriage, which was all the married life we had.

"Since that time, my love of the Egyptian countryside began. I saw the women as they carried goods on their heads, walking like dancing queens in their beautiful villages. I saw the village farmers in their traditional dress, the Galabiya, and their white head covers adding a beautiful aura of respect. I saw the fields like manicured green carpets arranged in beautiful crisscrossed landscapes. It was surely a holy picture.

"I loved the countryside from that moment, and that is where my love for the green color came from. If you look at those green fields extending as far as you could see, with trees of all types, flowers, and roses of all varieties and scent, you can add a vast array of fruit trees of all kinds to that. It felt like I was surely in heaven.

"Yet another surprise. I found a gorgeous royal golden boat anchored right in front of the palace on the beautiful Nile. At that time, my happiness grew more and more as I saw Farouk's kindness and affection, assuring me of his love. I was in paradise for two weeks, which represented my real happy life with Farouk. When we returned to Cairo, I prayed and prayed, thanking God for giving us those two wonderful weeks without interruption. It was our honeymoon.

"I didn't know that wars were waiting for me in Cairo. I began to confront those wars and uncover the secrets of the daily royal life. The jealously of Queen Mother Nazly, who did not appreciate Farouk's love for me, began to set in, fearful I might take him away from her. The arrows of vengeance overtly and covertly began to take aim at me with no letup. Since that day, while I was only seventeen years old, I began to feel that I had to confront these attacks that were focused on me, for no fault of mine except I was the king's wife.

"I began to respond to a whole series of infighting from the king's clans, his maids, and associates. There were all types of shameful acts, unbefitting a king, they wanted to control. I fought with everything I had, meeting their trickery and vengeful acts with as much patience and intelligence as I could.

"It quickly became clear to me that the actions of the king's court, his servants, and personal assistants were aimed at corrupting Farouk himself, keeping him preoccupied with trivial matters so they could take hold of governance and control of the Egyptian government. Once the conflict started between us, I was viewed as the obstacle in their way and the stumbling block in their path for achieving their goals.

"What was strange and astonishing to me was that they overtook Anshas, where I saw my best memories with Farouk. They began to use it as a hideaway for Farouk's party nights and a place for his sexual pleasures. The first to have the pleasure of using it was Madam Nahed Rashad. I learned later that Farouk kept a life-sized nude portrait of her on the wall of one of the palace rooms at Anshas.

"Sadly and even more ironic was that, after the Egyptian Revolution and deposing of Farouk, a group of officers went to inventory the palace and its contents. In their search inside the palace, they found Nahed Rashad's portrait, which they recorded as part of the palace inventory. So now, Nahed Rashad is nothing but an inventory item with the palace custodians."

Media Coverage of King Farouk and Queen Farida's Wedding in the Local and International Press

On the day of the wedding, Cairo's newspapers came out with full pages covering the celebrations. They showed pictures of the festivities that spoke volumes about the Egyptian people's love and affection to their king and queen. In *Al-Ahram* newspaper's coverage of January 20, 1938, it showed how the people celebrated their royal wedding. *Al-Ahram* described the wedding, saying, "Cairo was brilliant last night in her beautiful decor, and the scenes of her great joy, proud of the day and affirming that people's love for their king, is so deep in their hearts." The paper continued to report what the French newspapers published on the morning of January 19 about the events of the royal wedding celebration in Egypt.

At the same time, the French papers published many pictures of King Farouk and his bride, Queen Farida. *Media Paris*, the famed French newspaper, published an article under the heading "Tomorrow, Farida Zul-Faquar, shall be coroneted to the same royal crown that was Cleopatra's." The British newspaper, *The Scotsman*, published another article under the heading "A True Egyptian Girl." The article said, "Miss Farida exemplifies the ancient Egyptian femininity of her country. She is beautiful and fits as a wife to King Farouk . . . The new Egyptian generation is very optimistic in the future of their country and loves their young queen." The paper continued to offer its best wishes to Farouk, "who made the best choice in his queen" and to Miss Safinaz, "a name that projects elegance, purity, and beauty. Safinaz will now be known as Queen Farida. Her name, Farida, defines that simplicity, as is true of her personality. She'll hold a special position at the age of seventeen to be the youngest queen of modern times."

Farida makes the cover of Life Magazine on February 14th, 1938, in celebration of the Royal Wedding in Cairo.

The British Broadcasting Station Congratulates the Egyptian Community in London

At the Arabic-speaking British Broadcasting Station in London (BBC), the station pointed out the happy occasion of the wedding in Cairo. The BBC also broadcast a speech by Mr. Abdel Rahman

Hakky, *charge' daffier* of the Egyptian Consulate. In his speech, Mr. Hakky said, "The Egyptian people feel a great deal of kinship with the king as he chose their queen from his loyal subjects. With that, he has renewed a great and old tradition and gave a good example with his early marriage."

Abdel Rahman Hakky Beck, on behalf of the Egyptian community, congratulated the king and his bride and offered his heartfelt wishes of joy and happiness. "I am sure that Muslims in all of the Arab countries join the Egyptian people in their celebrations, and I would like to also thank our British friends and allies for showing this great regards to this happy and memorable event."

The *Daily Telegraph* published an article noting the reception that would be held at the Egyptian Embassy in London for the Egyptian community in England in celebration of the great royal wedding. On January 19, the London evening newspapers published descriptions of the great celebrations and equestrian dances performed in commemoration of the great royal wedding in Cairo.

Al Azhar students gathered in front of Abdeen Palace at Abdeen Square, chanting and celebrating in the king's honor. London's news media paid great attention in lengthy editorial coverage and pictures of the royal wedding between King Farouk and his young bride, detailing the typical Egyptian wedding traditions, the royal gown and all.

On Friday, January 21, the front page of *Al-Ahram* newspaper described the great affection the Egyptian people had for their king and their happiness with the royal wedding. It said in a poetic description of the event, "The earth blossomed with heavenly light, the world flourished with joy, and nature celebrated the wedding with its foremost beauty. The Nile streamed through the valley, its waves happily clapping and its waters serenading as they flow."

AlAhram News Paper Front Page coverage of
Farida's Wedding to King Farouk.

تهنئة

رفعة مصطفى النحاس باشا

رئيس الوفد المصرى

ان هذا القران الملكى السعيد ـ وهو أول زفاف ملكى فى مصر
الحديثة المستقلة ـ كان فرصة للشعب المصرى الوفى الكريم ، ليظهر فيه
بجميع هيئاته وطبقاته ما تكنه قلوبه من الاخلاص الشامل والولاء
الأكيد للملك الدستورى المحبوب ، وفى مقدمته الوفد المصرى ورئيسه
والوفديون الثابتون المخلصون ، وهم الغالبية الساحقة فى الأمة . وجميعهم
فى أفراحهم العامة ما برحوا يبتهلون الى الله العلى القدير أن يجعل هذا
القران السعيد طالع سعد للمليكين المحبوبين يحفهما التوفيق والهناءة
والخلف الصالح ، وللأمة الكريمة يفيض عليها الخير والاسعاد بالقضاء
على الدسائس الدنيئة لصالح البلاد

Nahas Pasha, the Head of the Wafd Party, congratulates
the King and the Queen on their Wedding, offering
their love and affection to the Royal Couple.

Alexandria Celebrates Our Wedding

Farida said, "Alexandria was among the most beautiful cities in the country, beautiful with the brilliance of its lights everywhere, the streets colorful with their decorations, and the streetcars draped in flowers and beautiful décor. Pictures of the king and the queen filled the street corners and squares. In droves, people went to the squares to listen to the Egyptian broadcasting stations announcing every bit of news about the royal wedding and detailing the news about the bridal parties all over the city. Even the Boy Scouts, local and foreign, came out in their beautiful uniforms. Army cadets marched in the streets, preceded by the National Guard's music bands and headed by the governor, chief of police, and other high-ranking officers.

"Ras-El-Tin Palace doors were open to delegations of Alexandrians of all professions and associations to sign special guest books specially prepared in commemoration of the wedding event. I remember the telegram declaration that the Alexandria scholars and notables sent to the chief of staff of the royal palace. In its congratulatory message, this very special telegram said,

'At this time, when the country is filled with joy and happiness, where people at every corner under the Egyptian skies are celebrating, let it be known that the head of the Alexandria Institute, its leading scholars, its employees, and students met at Ras-El-Tin Palace to send a proclamation of the most sincere congratulations to the honorable first lady, the queen, with our most solemn prayers. May God's blessings be with you and unto him. May you both be joined with most grace and happiness. Amen.'

The Wedding Gifts

When I asked the queen about her wedding gifts, she was quiet for a moment, recollecting her emotions. "We received lots of gifts at our wedding. My gift from the king was a precious necklace made of rare diamonds in three strings of white diamonds. At each end were diamond clips. Surely, this was a most beautiful piece, which was on exhibit at the international jewelry exhibit in Paris. I was so happy with it. It was certainly the most expensive gift I received.

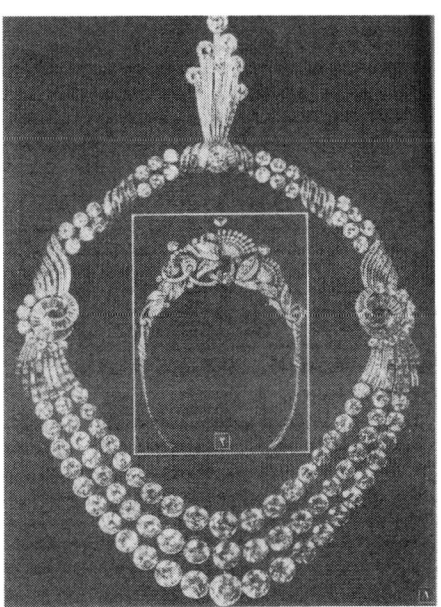

King Farouk's gift to Queen Farida, a most precious necklace, unmatched in its beauty and value at the time.

"Queen Mother Nazly, Farouk's mother, gave me a wedding gift, a crown laden with diamonds and a precious stone at the center. At the top of the crown, there was a heart-shaped diamond, and it was among the most precious crowns. This gift was a reminder of the beginning of my life and the first moments of my marriage.

"Farouk's family all shared in offering me a gift that was made up of a saucer and two cups made of solid gold, a very expensive gift. Diamonds and inscriptions decorated the plate. In the middle of the plate, the royal crown and King Farouk's name were beautifully engraved. In addition, each prince and princess brought his or her own wedding gifts for Farouk and me. Farouk gave me a personal gift of his own, a beautiful Mercedes that Hitler gave to him.

"From Austria, I received a group of statues representing the Austrian knights going back to the eighteenth century. Farouk received a gift from the king of Italy, an ancient bronze statue of an Italian prince from the seventeenth century. King George the sixth, the king of England, sent us a gift, two valuable hunting guns

The king of Greece gave us a bronze statue in the natural colors of the original statue kept at Athens' museum. Other gifts were received from the Arabian kings, which were primarily select beautiful Arabian horses from the kings of Jordan and Saudi Arabia."

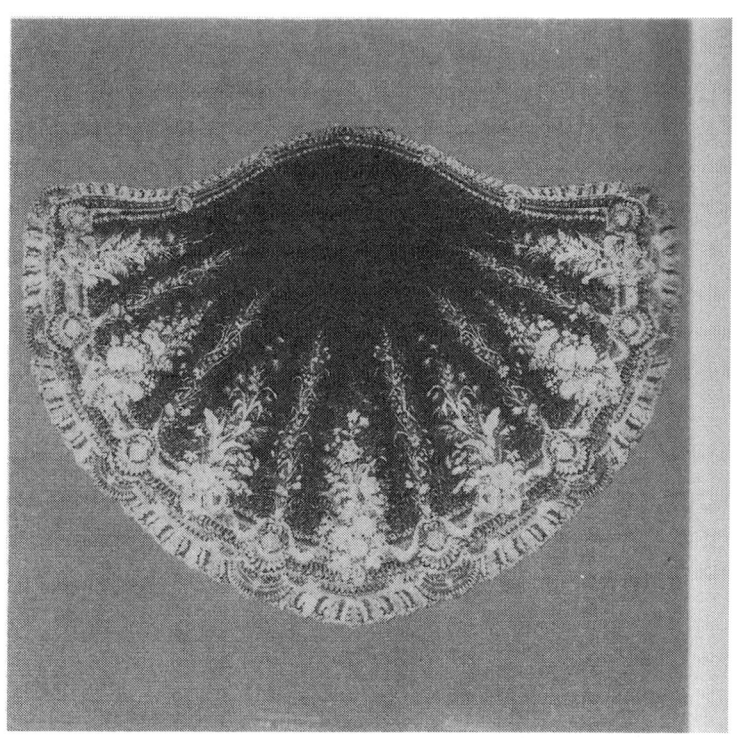

Rare gifts for the Royal couple from the kings and queens
Austria, Italy, Greece and from Prince Mohamed Ali Pasha.

The King and Almaraghy, the Struggle with the Wafd Party

The King's Coronation

Farida continued, "It started with a proposition by Sheikh Al Azhar, Sheikh Al Maraghy. Farouk had just taken the constitutional oath at the Egyptian Parliament. Sheikh Al Maraghy proposed that Farouk should be coroneted with his grandfather's Mohamed Ali's sward. This was to be performed in a religious ceremony at the Citadel. An enormous battle was unleashed between Al Wafd Party, which refused the proposal on one side, while the other political parties and Al-Azhar were on the other. I lived through this quagmire that actually started before my marriage to Farouk.

"It was clear from this conflict that Al Azhar was pushed into a political struggle. Al Azhar was used in such a marginal issue to capitalize on its spiritual power and people's respect for the institution and its leadership as well. Al Azhar became defiantly and unwillingly embroiled in a fight with Al Wafd and involved the king.

"At its roots, this conflict represented Al Maraghy's interest in promoting the idea of a religious coronation of the king when he ascended to the throne. The argument for that was based on the principle that the king inherits the throne by birth from his father and not through inauguration before the parliament. This was the issue, swearing in by the parliament on the one hand or the coronation by Sheikh Al Azhar on the other.

King Farouk and Sheik Al-Maraghy, Sheikh AlAzhar,
whose support was valued by King Farouk.

The King and Nahas Pasha, the Head of the Wafd Party, had conflicting views about the swearing in ceremony for the King.

Nahas opposed the idea of a religious Oath by the King for ascension to the throne, in lieu of the King taking the Oath in front of the Parliament. Nahas and AlWafd Party got their way and the King took the Oath before the parliament . . .

"With the help of his aides, Farouk kept an eye on Al-Maraghy, Sheikh Al Azhar. He wanted to win him to his side, as he was a spiritual and a political force for Farouk. Al Azhar was also an important element in fostering people's love and support of the king and their commitment to the throne. When Farouk was coroneted to the throne, everyone loved him. The Egyptian people had put their hopes and dreams in their beloved young king."

The queen continued to recall the religious coronation. "It was actually the idea of Prince Mohamed Ali, who demanded Farouk's religious coronation and supported Al Azhar and its leader, Al Maraghy, on that. Support also came from Sheikh Hassan Al-Banna, the leader of the Muslim Brotherhood. With that split, Al Wafd continued to refuse to abide by that order, and there was the beginning of the historical rift between Al Wafd and King Farouk.

"Support for the religious coronation came from what Al Banna intimated, 'At the time of the Caliphs, Muslims resorted to the Caliph in times of differences. Where he is now? We must all work to bring that to be.' These calls were supportive to the call for the religious coronation of Farouk, suggesting his assentation to the throne as a Caliph. Al Azhar and its leader, Sheikh Al Maraghy, welcomed the idea of religious coronation, worked to support it, and even called for it publicly. Furthermore, they proclaimed their support and loyalty to the king and the palace in their Friday speeches and sermon.

"The conflict deepened between the two camps, those supporting Al-Azhar's idea led by Sheik Al-Maraghy and Al Wafd and its supporters who were in opposition to it. The conflict was elevated to higher levels as the media got embroiled into it and the matter turned into a struggle for control between the young king and the Wafd Party with its influential leader, Prime Minister El-Nahas Pasha.

"The Wafd government insisted that the king could not be seated on the throne and become a constitutional king until he delivered the oath in front of the parliament. The prime minister's fear of the religious coronation was the essence of pushing religion into politics and using it as an attempt to create a religious authority that would compete with the civil authority of the government.

"In reality, Prime Minister Nahas' goal was not to give the king and the palace powers and to encircle the king's influence and not let him expand his authority. That was the first entanglement between the palace and the king and the Wafd Party. Nahas, the prime minister, indirectly got the people to come out in demonstrations supporting the Wafd, in defiance to the palace. The people's demonstrations came out, proclaiming their support to the government by their chanting, 'The people are with Nahas.' Similarly, the king coerced Al Azhar and Al Maraghy to initiate their own demonstrations, which were huge with Al Azhar students and the Muslim Brothers. In these demonstrations, all chanting slogans were 'God is with the king,' and the clash continued without abatement.

"There was another clash between the king and Al Wafd. After the religious coronation idea was defeated in favor of Nahas Pasha, the prime minster, the king appointed Ali Maher Pasha as his chief of staff without consulting the Wafd government. This was considered an incursion on the government's responsibilities. Al Wafd felt that Ali Maher was attempting to destroy the relationship between the king and the government. The king paid no attention to the objections of the government and kept Ali Maher as chief of staff.

"The conflict further escalated as the Al Wafd government pushed their troops with their characteristic blue shirts into Cairo streets, demonstrating their opposition to the king. At the end of 1937, Farouk issued a royal proclamation removing the Wafd ministry under the leadership of Nahas Pasha from the government. At the same time, the king appointed Mohamed Mahmoud Pasha to form a ministerial coalition from all the political parties with the exception of Al Wafd.

"In this environment was my marriage, but people of all persuasions and affiliations came out spontaneously and in great numbers, proclaiming their support to the king and chanting our names, the king's and mine, in their demonstrations. Farouk laughed, commenting on the coalition government, 'So that the Wafd does not get the exclusivity to our wedding as our marriage has become a national celebration.' As you can see, everyone—politicians, the common citizens, the army and the police forces, and all the Egyptian people—were sharing in our joyous celebrations."

Ali Maher, the Fox of Egyptian Politics

When I asked Queen Farida about Ali Maher, she said, "Ali Maher was a shrewd politician, and his influence on Farouk was strong and effective. When I married Farouk, Ali Maher was the chief of staff of the royal palace. Farouk's popularity was very high at that time. The people called Farouk the 'Beloved King.' Ali Maher was also known for his traditional animosity toward the Al Wafd Party. Actually, Al Wafd protested his appointment as chief of the royal staff, as I said earlier. Ali Maher was trained in the legal profession and acutely evasive in his dealings. As Farouk's chief of staff, Ali Maher played an important and effective role in directing the palace's political affairs and directed its dealings with the political parties and the British Ambassador. He was successful in many of his dealings, which earned him Farouk's confidence. Ali Maher was always on the side of the king, whether it was King Fouad or King Farouk. At the same time, Farouk learned a great deal in political matters and the ways of governance under the stewardship of Ali Maher.

Ali Maher Pasha, who mentored Farouk in many of his dealings throughout his tenure as the King of Egypt.

Ali Maher who attended to Farouk on his arrival from England to take the Oath after his father passed away.

Ali Maher was also the one who delivered the Revolutionary Council's ultimatum to Farouk, to relinquish his throne to his infant son on July 26th, 1952. Ahmed Fouad, Farouk's only son, was two years old at the time.

"Farouk learned so much from Ali Maher's trickery that he far exceeded his mentor. In his later days in government, it was astonishing to most people that Ali Maher complained about Farouk and his political dealings. It was a perfect example of a mentor whose student exceeded his own potential. Farouk appointed Ali Maher as prime minister several times during his rule of Egypt. The last of which was in January 1952 after the famous Cairo fires and just before the July 23 military revolution.

"As fate would have it, the man who taught Farouk the basics of politics at the time of his ascension to the throne was the same man who had Farouk sign his resignation from the throne fifteen years later. As Ahmed Hussein ruined Farouk's upbringing and his values, so did Ali Maher ruin Farouk politically."

Farida and the Incident of February 4, 1942

One evening, during a dinner at our house, Farida opened up the dinner conversation and started talking about many general matters. Taking advantage of the moment, I asked her, "Of course you lived through, as the king's wife, the famous incident of February 4, 1942? Much was written about that in the media, although with vastly different accounts. So tell me how you lived that experience? Do you have a special view of that day?"

My question startled the former queen, and she was visibly annoyed before she started to talk. Our surprise was that she started by saying, "The British insulted the king, the symbol of Egypt at the time, and that troubled me the most. Although my relationship with Farouk was going through difficulties, I was very taken by the incident.

"The wife of Mr. Miles Lampson, the British ambassador, visited me right after the February 4 incident, and with her was the wife of Mr. Leltoin, the British minister of state. They had each written a report about their meeting with me in which the ambassador's wife wrote,

'Farida was in a high state of nervousness and appeared troubled and very exhausted. She strenuously defended her husband while maintaining her composure about some of his actions and the actions of Queen Mother Nazly . . . Farida was very careful to bring her daughters up with a perspective of self-reliance. The queen also indicated that King Farouk was insulted in front of Egypt and the world. She expressed the displeasure of the Egyptian people for that.'

["The conflict that brought the British tanks and troops around Abdeen Palace was a conflict of wills. The will of the British occupation forces, through its representative Ambassador Miles Lampson, and that of King Farouk. The British Ambassador demanded the installation of the Wafd Party to lead the government after the Hussein Sirry Pasha government had fallen, but King Farouk would not accept the British demand. When King Farouk would not acquiesce, Mr. Lampson, put an ultimatum to Farouk to "either comply by six pm that day or face the consequences." It was also rumored that Mr. Lampson brought the document personally to the palace and, in asking to see the king, Lampson referred to Farouk as the "boy king". Farouk was twenty-two years old at the

time. Facing such embarrassment, King Farouk tried to not comply by the six o'clock deadline, but before the end of that day, he did comply and appointed Nahas Pasha to head the government. The conflict had more serious consequences as it not only undermined the king's authority but also damaged the standing of the Waft Party, well known for its opposition to the British occupation, to a party that was cooperating with them.

King Farouk and the British Ambassador Miles Lampson, who ordered the British troops and tanks to surround Abdeen Palace, threatening Farouk of his removal from the throne?

During World War II, a meeting between US President Roosevelt and King Farouk on board of a US warship.

Reports of the palace guard of that day documented their readiness to prevent an eminent confrontation with the British troops. The reports were signed by Colonel Ahmed Salem, chief of the Royal Infantry Guards; First Lieutenant Saleh Hassan Hosni, guard officer; Colonel Mohamed Moustafa El-Saharawi, royal aide; and Major General Abd-el-Hamid Bek Kamel, chief of the Royal Guard, who presented the reports in the Royal Guard archives. The reports documented all events that transpired from 8:55 through 21:05 on Wednesday, February 4, 1942."]

Farida continued with a de"ep sense of hopelessness. "I will not forget the British tanks circling Abdeen Palace. I will also not forget how sympathetic the Egyptian people were and how the army stood by the king after that incident. It was a golden opportunity for the king to bring the people around him, but unfortunately, he did not. Because the king returned to his usual behavior after the incident, the people—and the army with them—recognized that there was no hope in trying to bring him back to the right path and that matters had far surpassed him.

"After the February 4 incident, the princes and princesses competed in holding celebratory parties with all the excesses that can be imagined. It was as though they were trying to relieve some of the king's shock and anxiety after the incident. After all, Farouk saw the British forces surrounding the palace with full intimidation. They were forcing him to sign an abdication letter from the throne before he accepted the British ambassador's conditions and appointed Nahas Pasha to head the government, the main demand of the British.

"After that incident and the humiliation of the king, the symbol of the nation, I thought he would seize the moment and get closer to his people and the army. Unfortunately, Farouk's assistants and the rest of the Mohamed Ali royal family continued in their pursuit of partying to release the king's burdens. The parties continued under different hosts and in various places all over Egypt, from Al Marg to Anshas to Abdeen and in all the royal palaces inside and outside Cairo. The theme for these parties was to relieve the king's anxiety and depression.

"I felt that Farouk did not absorb the enormity of the lesson he had just been dealt. He was not mindful of the fact that the British, along with Al Wafd, were jointly preparing for his removal from the throne.

As such, instead of being cautious about the impending plans, Farouk resumed his life of parties and continued in the path that I believe was the beginning of his eventual fall. I urged him to go back to the army, but to no avail. All that was no barrier to Farouk's relapsing into his careless attitudes as he continued to indulge into his sexual fantasies and around-the-clock partying. It was the beginning of the destruction of the whole Mohamed Ali dynasty."

Farouk and Women

"When I married Farouk, I felt I was the happiest woman on earth. There he was, a young and handsome king who was loved by his people. He was loved to the point that, when his name was mentioned, it was always in conjunction with 'the beloved king.' People's happiness with him was just enormous. With all that, how else could I feel other than the love I had for him?

"On November 17, 1938, we were blessed with a beautiful daughter, whom we called Feryal after King Fouad's mother's name. I was so happy with her, but all those around me at the palace turned my happiness into tears. Everyone knew that Farouk's weak point was girls, as girls could not ascend to the throne. From that point, everyone started to play on that sensitive point that burned me over and over again.

"My burden grew deeper, as I was now responsible for giving him an heir to the throne. After each delivery, Queen Mother Nazly would tell me in front of the princesses and the maids; I got an heir to the throne for Fouad! let us see when will you bring an heir for Farouk. It was as if the matter was in my hands? They all forgot that it was in God's hands, not mine?

"My happiness was slowly being buried, and I felt deep sorrow, as all were demanding of me the heir to the throne. The most courteous of them would say, 'With God's will, next time you'll bring us an heir to the throne.' Every delivery became an unbearable pain. Before my delivery, I used to feel as if I were climbing the steps to be hanged. I had horrible feelings when I gave birth to my daughter Fawzyia, as everyone expected her to be a boy, the heir to the throne, but God willed it to be a girl. Fawzyia was born on April 7, 1940, and God willed Fadia to me on December 15, 1943. She was the last one God gave me and the one I loved the most of my girls.

"Before I had Fadia, all that was between Farouk and I was lost, and we became husband and wife in name only, as I gave up on giving birth to that elusive heir to the throne. I even thought of getting rid of my pregnancy, but my belief in God prevented me from doing that. The gap between Farouk and me began to widen. I began to see him only occasionally, and he would see me only at the girls' birthdays. I saw my life becoming aimless and meaningless. Farouk was always having late nights outside the palace, and if he came home, it was only to sleep.

"We began to avoid each other, and the distance widened between us by the day. I started to focus on raising my children while Farouk was absent most of the time. In essence, he became a husband in name only and absent in reality. The princesses began to ask about their father's absence, but I could not find any answers. This began to reflect on my emotional state, and a life of sadness began to surround my girls and me. I began to see sympathy in people's eyes and had to deal with inquiries that had no answers. I started to avoid leaving the palace for anything, whether it was to visit friends or relatives, and I stopped my social life. I hated to be among people who showed me false pretense that they cared while, deep inside, they were filled with deceit. They only cared about their own self-interest.

"Parties and receptions became mental burdens for me that I could not bear. These parties became façades and exhibitions toying with filth and lust, where people's honor was bought and sold and where the victims were surrendered to the king's pleasures. Even charity parties strayed so far from their intended honorable goals. Every girl and woman knew the failings in my husband's character, which was women, his ultimate fascination and enjoyment. I can frankly tell you that was the truth and Farouk did not try to overcome his own failings, especially his passion for women. His sexual desires preoccupied him, and that was my fate and the reason for my misery and ultimate divorce.

The Devil's Corner

"Princess Shwekar was the first wife of King Fouad. She was divorced from King Fouad because she could not get him an heir to the throne. The king later married Queen Mother Nazly, who brought him Farouk as the heir to the throne. Princess Shwekar did not forget what happened to her and kept holding her deep resentment and envy against Nazly. She used all possible tricks and revenge tactics to avenge the queen mother in her son Farouk. Shwekar planned and orchestrated every possible trick to ruin Farouk's character and make him the playboy that he became. With all of her intelligence and conniving, she planned parties under the name of Mohamed Ali's charitable organization while they did not have the slightest relationship to the cause. Quite the contrary, they were evil and corrupt in their own way. These parties were among the elements that brought down Farouk, destroyed him, and eventually dethroned him.

"Things began to work out for them, as Farouk got immersed more and more in his playboy life. His reputation was denigrated all over, locally and internationally. Farouk's immersion into the life of lust and filth kept him away from his responsibilities to his people. He was unresponsive to his duties to the nation, unaware of how harsh history can be when it judges rulers of nations. It was the royal corrupt clan, the tools behind all the evils that had befallen Farouk, and they were the strongest vehicle that led to his destruction. As God's words in the Quran say, 'Oh thee, who believe, do not take onto you, people below you; that they fill your imagination.'

"These wild parties were like show-and-tell, where gorgeous and beautiful girls paraded. Dancing to the tune of loud music, they wore almost nothing, but sheer covers exposed their luscious beauty and extreme desires. They would parade in front of Farouk while Shwekar would eye them for the most beautiful of them and the one with the best figure to send to Farouk. Almost like playboy bunnies, these girls were Egyptians, Italians, Greeks, Turks, you name it. They were there, ready and willing to be chosen for the king's pleasure but also to spite Farida, the queen, the king's wife! They were all there for the king to choose from for his sexual pleasures and fantasies.

"It was like Scheherazade's *One Thousand and One Nights*, only more lavish and boisterous. The drunken guests, the princes and princesses, the ambassadors, and society dignitaries were all having the nights of their lives as they watched this live parade of raw animalistic beauty before them. There was a stream of nude like and beautiful girls running to the boat docks and jumping into these man-made lakes on the palace grounds. There were no concerns to moralities, social responsibility, or any such thing but their human desires in its lowest form.

"Princess Shwekar, the symbolic owner of the Devil's Corner had a mysterious, almost sadistic, personality. She was married several times after her divorce from King Fouad, and each time, she would be divorced only to get married again and again. She was a specialist in arranging these loud, unrestricted parties with great food, music, dancing, wine, and liquor for all under the lavish lights of the Grand Palace, where they all gathered.

[1]Even at her age, Princess Shwekar fought Queen Farida, as though avenging her unhappy marriage to King Fouad many years earlier. The ensuing fights between Queen Farida and Princess Shwekar mounted to the highest levels, and the animosity between the two could not be hidden anymore, and war was declared between them. Everyone was trying to get the attention of the king and to pull him to her side. While Farida was trying to get him to be the model husband and father, caring for his wife and daughters, the king who needed to take care of his people's needs, he was nowhere, as though Farida was talking to herself. Shwekar, on the other hand, was making every effort to corrupt him.

Queen Farida told me, "Before the king and I had our difficulties, I used to attend and watch the preparations and rehearsals for the palace parties, which were done under the auspices of the Mohamed Ali Charitable Foundation. I used to participate and offer my comments and observations about these parties. I would even remove or change some of the segments, which I saw as unsuitable. Initially, Princess Shwekar would agree and implement my changes. After that, however, she began to complain to the king about my interventions and accuse me of being jealous or wanting to ruin the party's arrangements. With that, she managed to get a direct royal proclamation not to review these party arrangements with me."

---

1   *Princess Shwekar Hanem (1876-1947) was the cousin of King Fouad, Farouk's father. The two were married on May 30, 1895, at the Abbassiya Palace in Cairo. They had two children, a son, Ismail Fouad, who died in infancy, and a daughter Fawziya, who later married the Shah of Iran. Princess Shwekar's marriage was a particularly difficult one, especially after the death of their son. Shwekar was divorced in 1898, only three years after her marriage to King Fouad.*

"It actually went even further to the point that Farouk gave an explicit royal proclamation that I would not attend the rehearsals for the Mohamed Ali charity parties, that is, Shwekar's parties, which reached the highest possible levels of immorality and indecency. These parties used to remind us of the Russian parties that the Russian princes and princesses put together before the Red Revolution and the formation of the Soviet Union. Pictures of these parties were published in Tolstoy's book, *War and Peace*. Shwekar did not hesitate to arrange these parties. In fact, she always worked to organize them to advance her notoriety and stature on the public stage. The news and reports about the king's lavish parties spread like fire, not only locally in Egypt but also in Europe. Their news became front-page news in the many society magazines, locally and internationally. The king's parties were the envy of everyone who dreamed of being in the high society circles. It continued on a daily basis until the people became disgusted with the spoiled king. That was Shwekar's revenge, avenging Nazly by destroying her son Farouk. She prided herself in the society that she was closer to Farouk than his own wife and mother, Queen Mother Nazly, and that she could make him do whatever she wanted. Farouk was like a pawn under her spell, willing to do whatever Shwekar commanded. Those days saw the clashes between Shwekar and Nazly become stronger and stronger, each vying to get the king closer to her."

Camellia, "Lillian Cohen"

This chapter in Farouk's playboy book started when the king saw Camellia and admired her beauty. The first time was at *the Auberge des Pyramids* nightclub in Cairo. The king sent his emissary, Karim

Thabet, to invite her to his private quarters at the Abdeen Palace. In that meeting, Camellia was still high and intoxicated with alcohol, singing, dancing, and telling jokes to Farouk's laughter. Farouk liked her very much, and their relationship advanced so rapidly that he became so attached to her. The king wanted to take her on a romantic trip outside of Egypt. It did not matter to him what people said. It did not matter to him when people talked about the king's relationship with that Jewish girl who was controlling the king of Egypt.

So, Pulli, the king's personal assistant, arranged this romantic trip as a honeymoon where the king would live totally immersed in Camellia's passion. Farouk disappeared from the public scene, only to show up in Cyprus, the island of romance, under the factious name of Fouad Pasha, Al-Masry. There, in one of Cyprus's hotels, Camellia was waiting for him. Then the Associated Press announced the story of King Farouk's meeting with Camellia, which was immediately published, with pictures, in the foreign press.

When I asked Queen Farida about this incident and how she felt about it, she said, "You know I do not like to talk about these disgraceful events, but what saddened me more was that Farouk went on this trip without my knowledge or asking me to join him, even if it were just for a cover to such a disgraceful relationship. This trip contributed even further to his decline, as the newspapers and magazines wrote about it, and the matter became a subject of discussion and inquiry within the Egyptian cabinet. My birthday came and went without a note or even as much as a bouquet of flowers.

"Farouk did not care about all what was published about their meeting, and he actually went ahead and bought Camellia a villa on the Mountains of Rhoades after which Camellia came back to Cairo.

Farouk continued to frequent his visits with her and bought her a condo, which he chose for her, in Alexandria. Camellia also visited him in Cairo, and their relationship became well known and in the public view.

"The king arranged another trip for them in Europe, where he would meet her in Dovielle, France. But fate would not have them meet this time, as Camellia's plane fell out of the sky and crashed near Cairo on August 30, 1950. She was only twenty-one years old at the time of her death. Camellia's burned body was recovered at the crash site and identified. It was the body of Lillian Cohen, her real identity, although known as Camellia. With her death was the end of a sad chapter in this relationship between a Muslim king and a Jewish girl.

"It will never be known how much she was able to influence Farouk, as she succeeded in controlling his actions, getting him to follow her like a man with no will but to satisfy his passion and desires. She knew exactly what to do to get it; she was the expert. In the short period they knew each other, there is no telling of the extent of her influence over Farouk or the secrets that may have been passed to others through her. She had all the keys to his passion and the spark that lit up his dark soul. She became an enigma, unknown until today and leaving great many questions about their relationship.

"This unyielding passion came to the point that he would go on royal navy trips on his boat to the many ports of the Mediterranean to meet Lillian Cohen. She died taking with her all her secrets, leaving the most intriguing question of all was. Was she a Zionist spy? Was she advanced to the king's circle to uncover country's secrets? That was how much Farouk was undermined and how he became so corrupt and foolish to share the company of a Zionist girl, an enemy of the state."

The Palace Midnight Chase

One night after midnight, the queen noted a beautiful young and sexy girl walking in the hallways of the queen's quarters in the palace. She was later identified as Leila Sherine. Seeing her walking with her bare breast and exotic gown, Queen Farida quickly ushered her maid to catch up to her and bring her to her quarters. Leila Sherine confessed she had been with the king several times and she was the wife of an Egyptian. She was a dancer by profession and fond of acting. A formal inquiry was completed at the Abdeen police station for Leila Sherine.

The queen said, "That night, the king was not at the palace, as he was invited at Auberge El Fayoum, and the palace doctors considered the lady mentally deranged. The story quickly spread all over the palace. Since that day, I lost all hope in correcting Farouk's long and repeated stopovers outside the palace late at night, correcting his never-ending disgraceful actions. I had to ask for my divorce."

Queen Farida became emotionally distressed, and she was going through a difficult time to say the least. Shocked by her husband's actions, she was saddened for the deterioration of her marital relationship. In spite of the efforts she had done to protect the honor of her husband and family, the king continued to follow his crooked path that his Italian personal assistants painted for him. In the meantime, Queen Farida isolated herself on purpose and refused all invitations or attendance at any celebration, even official ones, and canceled her scheduled appointments. She lived in total isolation, not talking to or visiting anyone.

The queen insisted on divorce, no matter what happened, as she had seen the impossibility of living with Farouk after that. The king continued with chasing his sexual desires, not caring that it had ruined his public image in the country. It was almost as if he wanted it to be known without a care in the world.

The Queen and Waheed Yousry

After the scandal with Leila Sherine and her arrest inside the queen's quarters at Abdeen Palace, her confession was that she came on a previously arranged meeting with the king late that night. With her repeated accusation that she had been with the king several times before, she showed the king's ring as evidence of that relationship with him. These accusations stuck to the king, even when he was not present at the palace, yet causing the embarrassment that ensued about Farouk.

In response to this scandal and embarrassment for the king, revenge was in the offing, and the king wanted to embarrass the queen in the most urgent way. Taking opportunity of Queen Farida's visit to Princess Sameha Hussein, the wife of Prince Waheed Yousry, with whom she always found empathy and kindness, the king started to send his spies and guards to follow her everywhere she went. She used to make these visits without the king's knowledge, which gave him more reason to send his detectives after her.

Even though the king had all the trust in Queen Farida, he manufactured a story from his sick (diabolical) mind and accused her of having a relationship with Waheed Yousry. The king himself went to Princess Sameha Hussein, asked her to stop seeing the queen, and told her that there was an affair between the queen and her husband. The princess quickly refused the request and continued to see Queen Farida and receive her at her home.

After that, the queen confided in me that, even after Princess Sameha Hussein refused the king's request, she began to feel a subtle change in the way that the princess received her. The princess' usual kind reception and sharing of emotions had suddenly stopped. She did not know if that was due to Sameha's jealousy for her husband, fear of the king's trickery, and his capacity for revenge or if she believed his accusations. The princess was in fact concerned for her husband and the king's possible revenge. It was not clear whether that change was because of the princess' jealously or actual fear of Farouk. With that, Waheed Yousry did not escape Farouk's troublemaking.

Queen Farida saw that the palace that gave her peace and comfort had turned its back on her. She never thought that Farouk, who knew of her purity and decency, would stoop to that level and try to damage her reputation using this fictitious story. His cohorts, his evil Italian personal assistants, who were envious of Queen Farida, made up these stories, and they wanted to get rid of her at all cost. Farida had declared war against them as soon as she knew that they were the ones who accompanied the king every night to the nightclubs and houses of disrepute.

During their troubled times, Farida would insist that Farouk fire his Italian associates, and the king would promise to be rid of them gradually. However, when he failed to keep his promises, she asked for divorce. The king's maids and their associates saw an opportunity in Farida's situation to create even more troubles, as they knew very well how she felt about them and their influence on Farouk. They also found a great partner in Queen Mother Nazly, who shared in their animosity to Farida. They began their mischiefs and troublemaking for Farida and declared a vicious war against her, taking full advantage of the king's misperception about Farida and

Prince Waheed Yousry. They made up an unbelievable and untrue story, a case against Farida. They followed her everywhere she went; they sent spies after her to collect any damning evidence. They failed to find or gather any such damaging information, as all the stories they concocted were untrue. Knowing Queen Farida's character and purity, no one could believe their stories.

Despite all of that, the king and his clans continued to push the story that Queen Farida was in a romantic relationship with Prince Waheed Yousry, especially that Farida would not stop visiting her friend Sameha Hussein. If she did, that would confirm the rumors rather than dispel them, so Farida did not.

The Royal Couple, King Farouk and Queen Farida,
with their first-born Princess Feryal.

Two Queens and One Palace

Nahed Rashad

As if all that was happening was not enough pressure on Queen Farida, fate would have it yet again that another lady would show up in the king's life, and again, he would fall in love with her. That was Nahed Rashad, the wife of the king's personal physician, Doctor Youssef Rashad.

As the story went, it started when a collision with the king's car occurred at the town known as Al Kassassin. Responding to the scene of the accident was Dr. Youssef Rashad. When Dr. Rashad arrived, he carried the king to the hospital and took care of him throughout his treatment. He stayed very close to the king. After which, the king appointed him as his personal physician. Nahed Rashad used to come to visit her husband, Youssef Rashad, at the palace. Not long thereafter, the king took note of her presence and fell madly in love with her. He appointed her as an assistant to his sister, Princess Fawzyia, and assigned a bedroom nearby for her use. She became the uncrowned queen in the palace for her enormous influence on the king. She was beautiful, tall, and elegant with her beautiful long hair and aggressive character. She was unstoppable in her influence around the king. She became his constant companion in all his outings and nightly parties. Queen Farida began to boycott all these parties, as Farouk had no shame and would flirt with Nahed Rashad, even in the presence of her husband.

At one point, Queen Farida said, "On one occasion, at the Romance Nightclub and in the presence of Farouk's sister, Princess Fawzyia, and in view of all present, the king placed a red rose in Nahed Rashad's bare cleavage with his own hand. It got even worse when he rented a private condo in Giza and started to spend most of his nights with her there. As Farouk's sexual desires controlled his actions, he became so attached that he could not leave her even for a moment. He had a life-sized portrait made of her in the nude and hung it on the wall at the Anshas Palace. Her nude portrait remained on the palace wall until the revolution of 1952. That portrait became an inventory item among the palace contents when the Revolutionary Council's auditors ceased it.

"Farouk's relationship with Nahed Rashad grew closer and closer, and she began to accompany him on his foreign trips. She actually thought she might indeed become the queen of Egypt. In advancing that goal, Nahed Rashad did everything she could to poison my relationship with Farouk. Even more so, she was intent on destroying all the remaining bridges between the king and me."

With deep sadness, the queen continued in her soft voice, "The situation had deteriorated to the extent that Farouk became the talk of the town, and the society women were all betting on his next love affair" . . . " They were, sorry to say, not real ladies, but prostitutes and men chasers who were hungry for money and fame if they connected with the king. Even the elite of the society women were vying for their moment of fame, their moments in the limelight with Farouk."

Queen Farida was saddened as King Farouk became more and more the object of women's folly, especially those who saw their opportunities to be the queen of Egypt, thinking they were more worthy of the crown than she was.

"The king's entourage and his corrupt personal assistants made it their duty to keep pushing these types of women on him. They would send them to the nightclubs that he frequented, spending whole nights in these clubs and cabarets, drinking and dancing with no concern to anything, especially to his position as the king of this wonderful country. You can imagine how a wife, not even a queen, could stand for all this, witness all the scenes, hear all the rumors about her husband, and see him ridiculed by all the women chasing that he did.

"I can remember how they coerced some of my maids, whom I trusted as friends, to come and tell me stories about Farouk and his women. I now know that it was not to console me or provide empathy, but in fact, it was to avenge me and destroy my body and soul. At the same time, it was their way of proving to me that Farouk would never return to his early days and he had in fact reached the end of his line, that he would never come back to his daughters or me. I was angry, not just for myself my daughters and my family, but for Egypt. Farouk became the victim of the evil currents that shaped his actions and made him such a disgraced king."

The King and the Devil's Court

"Farouk was raised among the maids and servants of the palace. He lived all his life from birth to death with great admiration of the West. Being so young and impressionable, Farouk did not know or appreciate the fact that he was the ruler of the oldest country in human civilization. His travels to Europe left great influences on his life, ones that reflected greatly on his personal behavior. He adopted many of the traditions and behaviors of the Western society, especially sexual freedom and promiscuity. That made him driven by his sexual fantasies and lust for women throughout his life. It was like a disease that he had in needing women so much. This was in stark contrast to the life in the Eastern societies where cultural and religious norms bind people. These norms were the products of thousands of years of traditions that ultimately controlled their actions and ruled their behavior.

"There is no doubt that there are enormous differences between Eastern and Western cultures, the way they live, the extent of personal freedom, and the limitations, or lack thereof, that shaped these societies and their values. Add to that Farouk's upbringing surrounded by the palace maids and personal assistants who helped mold his personality. Much of the environment he grew up in was the influence behind his actions and defined his moral compass for the most part. The Italian and Greek assistants held the reins on him so tight, like a heavy pendant on his neck. They became the vehicle of control over his actions that they were referred to as the 'devil's circle that cannot be broken.'

"In the June 16, 1939, *Al Mouswar* magazine, Fikry Abaza, the magazine editor at the time, who later became editor-in-chief of *Dar Al Helal*, characterized the palace maids and assistants, saying,

'It is that clan that holds onto the king; surrounds him at all times, his work time, his spare time, his fun, and pleasure; calling onto him and he onto them, away from his formal duties and obligations. They are the ones who brought him the information, arranged for him the day's events, broadcast his affairs, created the rumors, encouraged or consoled him, and ushered him to the right or the wrong paths.'

"You may note in this characterization that Abaza was exposing and admonishing the king's clan with his well-known subtle articulation. The king lived his childhood surrounded by the servants and assistants who were accustomed to blindly obey him while using that to achieve their own goals and aspirations. That upbringing and loose environment made him an arrogant, stubborn, and decadent man. Farouk did not know how to take advice or to evaluate his actions. He only cared about carrying out his wishes, like a child irrespective of all else around him."

The Palace Electrician, Antonio Pulli (Beck)

In 1922, at the time of King Fouad, an Italian electrician in the palace knew Farouk since his early childhood, actually since he was born. This was Antonio Pulli, who befriended Farouk throughout his early years and became very close to him. Pulli, using all the tools at his disposal, eventually became responsible for all the king's affairs and became his personal confidant. Pulli used to introduce women to Farouk, and Farouk trusted him so much. Pulli's influence on Farouk was unmatched by anyone else at the palace. In fact, he ended up living in the king's quarters, and it became impossible for anyone to have access to Farouk except through Pulli. He became like the king's shadow, going with him anywhere and everywhere he went, day or night. The British hated the Italians with Pulli on top of the list and feared his great influence on Farouk. In fact, the British tried to remove Pulli from the king's inner circle through their ambassadors, Sir Miles Lampson and Lord Clarin. This was because of Pulli's increasing influence and becoming a constant companion to the king, even during formal functions. As expected, the British efforts against Pulli failed. He also had great influence on the king's trade transactions and his uncanny financial dealings. Pulli was also accused in the faulty weapons deal when the army procurement office purchased a large cash of weaponry that later proved defective during the Arab–Israeli war of 1948. Even there, Farouk was able to clear Pulli of that."

Queen Farida told me about her experience with the Italians, as there were many under Pulli's leadership. "They worked around the king and acted precipitously to undermine his powers throughout his rule. Several of them were working under Pulli, of whom I remember, Petro and Fritch. When I left the palace, twenty of them formed the base of corruption around the king. I used to call them 'the devil's court in the palace.'"

Queen Farida abhorred the British occupation and hated the manners of the British ambassador, who used to refer to Farouk as the "boy king." However, she understood that the reason for Farouk's corruption was because of his Italian clan that filled the palace and spread everywhere and in all positions of influence at the palace. The British government and its ambassador did not trust the Italian personnel at the palace under the leadership of Pulli. They were suspicious of their roles as spies for the enemy, passing on the movements of the British forces when they were approaching the Western desert during WWII. However, Pulli's primary responsibility was the pleasure of King Farouk."

Queen Farida understood that those Italians came from a Western society, not an Eastern one. She knew they were transforming the king as they manipulated his nightlife at the nightclubs, losing sight of his family, his children, and his country's affairs. "That reflected, in the eyes of the Egyptian people, on the value of the family unity and structure and contributed to his mismanagement of the country's affairs. It affected people's view of him as a ruler and a model leader to emulate.

"When I demanded that the king get rid of them, his response was to give Pulli the honor of the title Beck. What is worse was that when the British asked for their expulsion, Farouk answered back by giving all of them the Egyptian citizenship. It may be said that the devil's court was responsible for much, if not all, of Farouk's personality failings. It paved the way for his downfall, eventual expulsion, and loss of the throne."

The Palace Ruler, the Servant Mohamed Hassan

"Mohamed Hassan, a Nubian known as Shamarshagy, worked as a janitor at one of the Egyptian shops before he joined the palace staff. Upon joining the palace house personnel, he became the personal servant of the king. In no time, Mohamed Hassan became the link between the king and his chief of staff. Later on, he also became Farouk's link with the prime minister. Mohamed Hassan became so influential that he would respond to and put his own signature on the king's formal correspondences. With that, Mohammed Hassan became the true ruler of the palace and a symbol of the servant's rule during Farouk's governance of Egypt. As it were, Mohamed Hassan, the Nubian servant; Pulli and Garro, the king's barbers; Pietro, the barber's assistant; and Kafateth, the dog's trainer, became Farouk's best and most trusted friends in the palace.

"That was the devil's troops. The people who ran the king's personal affairs attended to his pleasures, accompanied him to the places he frequented, brought him the girls, and satisfied his personal desires at all the nightclubs they could find. Auberge Al Haram, the Automobile Club (AAA), and Helmeiah Palace, among others, were where Farouk spent his time away from the palace, away from his wife and daughters and his duties as the king of Egypt."

The Private Chauffer, Mohamed Helmy Hassanien's Promotion to an Army Colonel

"The private chauffer for Farouk, Mohamed Hassanein, was an enlisted army corporal. He taught Farouk how to drive when he was a young boy during King Fouad's rule. When Farouk became the king, he promoted his chauffer to the rank of colonel and appointed him as the general manager of the royal fleet. That was the publicly announced position, but in fact, he was an ardent competitor to Pulli. Mohamed Hassanein also got into Farouk's favorite few, joining in finding and bringing women for the king.

"Later on, Mohamed Hassanein was given the title Beck and came into untold wealth through weapons trade deals. The palace connection helped him procure for the army's major weapons deals. The king used to send him on official visits to the extent that he would send him as a personal emissary, delivering messages to heads of states and governments of the Arab countries."

The King's Promoter and Poet, Kareem Thabet

"Kareem Thabet was another man of influence on Farouk's life. A Lebanese Christian, Kareem Thabet had a great personal impact on Farouk's emotional being and psyche. The king knew Kareem Thabet when the king and I were on a trip to Aswan in 1942. Kareem Thabet knew how to capture Farouk's attention when we were at the Cataract Hotel in Aswan. He started to weave his controlling network around Farouk by constantly praising him. He just kept praising Farouk at every possible occasion until Farouk appointed him as his media advisor in 1946. His influence began to deepen, and his reach expanded that he began to join the king everywhere he went, his nightly excursions and all. Knowing Farouk's weakness toward women, Kareem Thabet too began to extend his services to the king that Farouk became like a pawn in his hands and to move wherever he wished.

"The king subsequently gave him the title of Beck and followed by the title of Pasha. He then appointed him in Hussein Serry's cabinet as a minister of state toward the end of his rule. Thus, Kareem Thabet became a major architect in the corruption of the palace and, along with his wife, became a strange combination. He too accumulated enormous wealth and a great influence on Farouk. I remember Kareem Thabet's name being mentioned in the weapons corruption case as well. His wealth grew through his ownership of high-rise apartment buildings in Cairo and Alexandria and stocks in major corporations, along with money in the banks. He became among the wealthiest of Egyptians."

The Chief of Staff, Ahmed Hussein Pasha

"Ahmed Hussein was another in a long list of characters who played major roles in the life of King Farouk. Ahmed Hussein's involvement, however, started much earlier in Farouk's life. It started when King Fouad entrusted him to accompany Farouk to England to finish his education and to be his teacher and mentor. On October 6, 1935, Farouk went to England on a British destroyer and arrived in London on October 18 of that year. Farouk stayed at the country House Palace, and he had not reached his sixteenth birthday at that time. At such a critical age, Ahmed Hussein was in a position to mold Farouk any way he wanted. Since then, Farouk got into the nightlife and the company of women at such a young age.

"Farouk became known in London as the 'adolescent prince.' Ahmed Hussein had also received his education in England. He attended Oxford University and got much of his lifestyle, education, and tradition from living in England for several years. He let Farouk be on his own, opening the doors far and wide for a young, impressionable adolescent to pursue his personal pleasures. It surely was a bad beginning, as it offered Farouk the opportunity to live as an adult at such a young age. Ahmed Hussein forfeited the trust that was given him by King Fouad as a teacher and mentor for Farouk. An impending clash was to take place soon thereafter between Ahmed Hussein and Aziz Al Masry.

"Aziz Al Masry, a respected Egyptian military man, was sent to England to mentor Farouk in his militarily education and training. He was quite the opposite of Ahmed Hussein. As a military man, Aziz Al Masry was organized, disciplined, and nationalistic. He felt that Farouk should be brought up in the military tradition adhering to his national principles and traditions. He felt that Farouk's manner of upbringing should be a serious one, adhering to the Islamic traditions and being a role model for all Egyptians as an honorable Muslim king.

"As the two mentors, with their opposing views on character building, tried to direct Farouk their way, Ahmed Hussein pushed him into the pleasurable and playboy lifestyle, spending all of his time in the nightclubs, while Aziz Al Masry looked at instilling moral principles and responsibility. The two clashing perspectives started to show their impact on Farouk. In the meantime, Ahmed Hussein was focusing his plans to take over Farouk's future for his own benefit after Farouk was crowned as the king of Egypt.

"Aziz Al Masry, recognizing that Farouk had become infatuated with the nightlife and having all but lost his focus on education, living the lifestyle of alcohol and sex, which Ahmed Hussein had paved, decided to return to Egypt. He left London to exonerate himself from the failings in Farouk's character. Farouk had actually begun to be annoyed with Aziz's advice and attempts to put him on the right path of decency and responsibility.

"After King Fouad passed away, Farouk came back to Egypt in the company of his great mentor and teacher, Ahmed Hussein. By that time, Farouk had become like a toy that had been molded in the manner Ahmed Hussein wanted. As if that were not enough, Ahmed Hussein went even further establishing a covert relationship with Queen Mother Nazly and marrying her secretly in a civil marriage ceremony. Ahmed Hussein was actually still married to Ms. Latifa

Yousry, the daughter of Princess Shwekar. This amazing triangle may also explain the origin of the war that ensued between Nazly and Shwekar.

"As you can see, Nazly's marriage to Ahmed Hussein gave her the opportunity to tighten her reins around Farouk, making Ahmed Hussein the uncrowned king ruling Egypt from behind the scenes. Fate will have it, as the final arbiter in these life matters, Ahmed Hussein died in 1947 as a result of a car accident, leaving Nazly and Shwekar for their infighting around Farouk and the palace."

When I asked Queen Farida about Ahmed Hussein's role in Farouk's early life, she said, "Ahmed Hussein was the perfect example of a man who lived only for himself, one who did not care about anything or anyone except for what was good for him and him alone. He was the kind of a person that you really did not know what his objectives were or where he was going with his devious planning. He was also simple and very diplomatic. He always appeared polite, kindhearted, and soft spoken. He believed in the Machiavellian principle that the end justifies the means. He was a great believer of that school and able to get whatever he wanted in any way or by any means that were at his disposal.

"Farouk, at the beginning of his rule, used to listen blindly to Ahmed Hussein and follow his advice and directions. He acted as if he were running the country and the Egyptian political affairs. At one point, however, when that relationship soured, Farouk would not hear of him or the mention of the name Ahmed Hussein again."

The Queen and Palace Corruption

Queen Farida began to feel the difficulties in her life. Her unhappiness became unbearable, and she could no longer stand up against the king or his foolish behavior—King Farouk's continuous nightly stands at the nightclubs and cabarets, his constant drinking and gambling, and his nightly stints outside the palace among those who had no care except for their own benefits and pleasures. She wished so many times to leave all the palaces, the maids, and assistants just to live a simple life where she could have a peaceful life with her family, her daughters, and husband, King Farouk.

The king tried to reduce Farida's anxiety and buy her silence so she would not continue complaining about his corrupt court. He gave her gifts and jewelry, but she would not stop. One of Farouk's gifts, or bribes for her silence, was two thousand acres of land called Al-Farida Ranch, named after Queen Farida. This ranch was in the governorate of Sharkyia. But as I knew Queen Farida, she was not the kind of person who could be bought or swayed against her will in any direction at any price. Gifts, money, or even a two thousand-acre ranch could not buy her silence, as she continued speaking her mind and pointing out the palace corruption that was rampant everywhere in the palace. Queen Farida was proud, self-confident, and keenly aware of her rights and responsibilities. She let all those around her know that her silence could not be bought, not for all the gold in the world.

She grew more resistant to Farouk's intimidation, unyielding to his tactics that did not change her mistrust of him. Though he was the one whom she loved dearly during the days and months of their engagements and for the first few years of their marriage, it did not continue without the greatest of sacrifices, be that on her emotions or her pride and almost her sanity.

She determined that Farouk had reached the point of no return for her and felt she had failed in trying to correct his behavior or clear his reputation. He abandoned his wife and daughters and spent most of his time outside the palace and in the company of his lovers and associates. Farouk began to act like the adolescent he was in his youth, spoiled by Shwekar and all those who needed him for their fun and joy.

Al Tahra Palace

Many people in Egypt may not know that Al Tahra Palace, which means the "Palace of the Pure One," located in the El-Zaytoon suburb of Cairo, was named after Queen Farida. The story began when Farouk offered the palace to Queen Farida to buy her silence about his corrupt clan at the palace. It was another gift and another attempt by Farouk to stop Farida's nagging requests against his Italian court. He thought that would give her privacy and keep her out of the palace affairs.

The king went with Queen Farida to this grand palace, an unparalleled architectural marvel made with the best Arabesque décor and beautifully furnished with a mix of French, Turkish, and Persian furniture. Paintings and artworks from the Middle Ages decorated the palace's walls and beautiful ceilings. It was as grand as any palace one sees in Europe, particularly the old castles in France.

Farouk, seeing how impressed Queen Farida was and how much she liked the palace, told her, "I'll give it to you as a present." The king then forced his cousin, Prince Mohamed Taher, to sign a deed relinquishing his ownership of the palace for a mere forty thousand Egyptian pounds. The king named the palace Al-Tahra Palace for the queen's purity. He deeded the palace in her name, in appreciation of her nobility and honorable character.

Some said that Farouk offered this palace to Farida so she would stop focusing on his relationship with his Italian servants and assistants, not understanding that could never dissuade Farida from her attempts to rescue him from those evildoers, those whom she called the "devil's troops."

Even though the king kept promising to get back on the straight path, he never had the intention to do so, nor to actually commit to doing it. After a while, the king simply ignored Farida's advice and went on with his pleasures and hanging out with the same people who would eventually cause his ultimate demise and exile in disgrace.

The queen was never a deceived wife. At no time during her marriage was she oblivious of what was happening around her or what the king was doing in front of her as well as behind her back. Nor was she accepting the ridicule that Farouk was continually exposed to in front of everyone. She was intelligent, vibrant, and full of life to her last day.

The Last Confrontation, "The Confession"

Continuing to remember the early days of her marriage, Queen Farida said, "In light of all what happened between Farouk and me, I decided I must confront him with all I held inside. I wanted to tell him face-to-face and for the last time about all the things that kept us apart.

"It was 1945. That year, I learned a great deal about what was going on inside and outside the palace. I learned about the things that were hidden from me. During that period, I noticed that Farouk could not, or maybe would not, listen to my suggestions. When I merely pointed out simple concerns to Farouk or politely raised issues with him, he became angry. That was not how Farouk was before. Initially, we were able to discuss matters between us without anger. We did not always agree, but he would politely acquiesce while not doing anything about it. They were, nevertheless, civilized arguments.

"At that point, it became clear to me that it was no longer useful or effective in getting his attention to make changes. It was not the first time that I tried to confront Farouk and let him know that I could never stand to his actions and embarrassments. I was always alert to his actions, quick to point out his faults and personal failings, sometimes in a calm manner and, at other times, with my anger and hurt fully expressed and vented. He was also a very stubborn man who did not listen to my complaints or arguments.

"I was hoping for a kind and gentle husband and a caring father, but that was not to be. In the first few years of our marriage, he listened to me and explained his actions. He would claim that they were unintended, those rumors were not true, or 'those who gave you the information are liars and do not know what they were talking about.' He made excuses that were not believable. However, as a wife, before being a queen, I wanted to hold on to my marriage, my husband, and my family life. That was very important for me to hold on to.

"When all else failed and our marital difficulties became public knowledge across town and the country, when the scandals were reported in the local and foreign media, it became clear to me that my silence was tantamount to my acquiescence and acceptance. It appeared to those who did not know me that I was accepting this humiliation for the crown or I was silent and persevering to stay in the palace. But those who were close to me knew well that I was not the kind who would tolerate all that for the life of luxury or the palaces that were actually mine. Even the crown also belonged to me as the queen of Egypt. All did not matter as much as my longing for a real honest-to-goodness simple family life with my daughters and a loving husband. Not having any of that, I insisted on getting my divorce.

"I had to bear what mountains could not, fight the pressures and humiliations that no one could take. I tolerated all that for many years. I did not give up after the first clash or the first fight, but I kept fighting for myself, my husband, and my daughters. When it was no longer possible to change Farouk, especially in the midst of his evil partners whose primary occupation was to keep him drunk and keep supplying him with women for his pleasures, it was obvious that I could not carry that burden any longer, and I continued to insist on my divorce. I insisted with full conviction that divorce was the only way. Farouk had become intolerable and impossible to deal with. He simply had reached the end of the line with me. He had damaged his character beyond repair. He lost all of his principles and became fixated on one thing and one thing only, his desires. He lost his respect among his people and became like a toy in the hands of his Italian servants and associates. They came to the point of influence to arrange his schedule as they pleased.

"I insisted on getting my divorce until I actually got it, a process that took almost three years of my insistence. I left the palace that

I once cherished and hoped to raise my children in the comfort of a loving husband and a caring father for my daughters, but that was not to be, and I accepted my fate."

I Asked for My Divorce Because I Loved Farouk

The queen told me, while she was deeply immersed in her sad memories, "I asked for divorce because I loved Farouk, and I wanted so much to keep all my memories deeply tucked in within me, as though they were going to evaporate and disappear."

Queen Farida began her last phase with Farouk by boycotting all official functions. She stopped joining the king in his ceremonies, whether they were official or private. She was extremely stubborn when it came to matters that touched her honor and her ideals. "The king chose a specific time for accepting my demand for divorce. He did not want to have my divorce circulated among the Egyptian people in any public way. He accepted my demand on the condition that it would be at the same time as his stepsister Princess Fawzyia's divorce.

"Princess Fawzyia was married to the Shah of Iran. She was also in the process of getting her divorce from the Shah. Farouk took all the precautions so there would not be a major reaction to my divorce in Egypt or the Arab world and especially the Muslim world. The divorce became official on November 17, 1948, almost eleven years after we got married on January 20th, 1938. The official divorce pronouncement was made on the same day of the divorce decrees announcing my divorce from Farouk and Princess Fawzyia's from the Shah of Iran."

Queen Farida returned to her father's home with her youngest daughter, Princess Fadia, and the king insisted that Fadia would go back to him if Farida remarried. The king used his close relationship with Sheikh Al Maraghy, the head of Al Azhar, to try to make a religious proclamation that she could not get married again. Al Maraghy would not accept his request and declined to make such a proclamation, or a fatwa. Al Maraghy knew it was contrary to Islamic Sharia to make such a fatwa.

"Farouk continued to pressure Al Maraghy to make another fatwa to prevent me from seeing my daughters, but again, Sheikh Al Azhar would not succumb to the king's pressures and refused to make proclamations that were contrary to Islamic laws. Farouk tried for a third time to have Al Maraghy make a proclamation that would deny me the right to get married again, but once more, his demands were rejected flat-out. Sheikh Al Maraghy stood by me all throughout my divorce proceedings. He was my protection against the harshest demands of the king, to the extent that he actually suffered from Farouk's frustration and anger later on. Sheikh Al Maraghy, Sheikh Al Azhar, was a great man in the true sense of the word. He was a Muslim leader the likes of whom Egypt had not seen since. He stood by me and against the king because what Farouk asked for was against the basic Islamic tenants. This was at a time when no one else helped me through my most difficult time.

"It was rumored that, when Sheikh Al Maraghy passed away, Farouk came to his house and asked all present to leave him with Sheikh Al Maraghy's corpse. After Farouk left the room, the family noted that the king had stolen Sheikh Al Maraghy's personal notes that was left next to his body. These notes were no longer there after the king left the room. Farouk clearly did not want anyone to see or read what the Grand Sheikh might have written about our divorce in his personal notes during the last period of his life.

"Before my divorce from Farouk, everyone—friends, relatives, and family members—used to ask me to just look the other way at the corruption that was going on. I was repeatedly cautioned that that was the way kings and royalties lived and to just accept it. I could not trade my honor, my daughter's lives, and the dreams I had for a peaceful and honorable life for a life in a wicked and corrupt palace, one that was turned into the whore house that it was, a house that an evil group of people who took over Farouk, body and soul, ran. After the divorce, I took back my original name Safinaz, took my youngest daughter Fadia, and moved to my father's house. People's reactions to the news of the divorce were expressed in sadness and polite displeasure with the king."

With that divorce, Farouk lost a great deal, as the people loved Farida. She was always noted for her honorable stands and fighting for the people's rights and their respect. The people knew that, after Farida left the palace, it would turn into the devil's house with all the gambling, drinking, sex, and corruption, which did resume.

She talked to me about her life after being dethroned and living in the palace that Farouk gave her as a gift after the divorce. "That palace was beautifully situated at the foot of the pyramids by the Nile." She remembered sitting every day on the terrace, totally quiet, looking in front of her at Egypt's Nile and the pyramids, both representing the history and grandeur of Egypt. They were also the symbols of the greatest ancient civilization the world had ever known. Those silent moments of reflection would etch into her memory the pictures of the simple Egyptian people who had given, time and again, through history to the world since Pharaonic times. The Nile view recorded in her memory the images of the beautiful Nile trips she had with King Farouk in the early days of their marriage. She reflected on how the Nile sustained Egypt, keeping its legacy as invaders came and left. She saw, in her mind's eye, how Egypt's Nile witnessed all of its seven thousand years of history and how it still continues to flow in front of her, day in and day out.

Marriage Proposals after the Divorce

The queen confessed to me that, after her divorce from Farouk, she received a great many offers of marriage. "These offers came with enormous gifts and promises of wealth. My answer was always no. I simply could not see myself after being the queen and first lady of Egypt to be remarried to anyone else. In fact, in 1963, I had to leave Lebanon, where I resided for a while, because of the continued insistence of one its wealthiest people in asking for my hand in marriage. I simply left the whole country to avoid such requests, which became almost like demands.

"Deep inside, I felt I did marry King Farouk, but I was not successful in securing my life with him. That feeling made me believe that I could not repeat that episode once more and I had to be resigned to that fate."

Farouk's Luck Runs Out after Farida's Departure

For a while, it looked like Farida brought King Farouk luck with her when they got married on January 20th, 1938. As soon as Farida left the palace, the world came tumbling down on Farouk. It looked like all the problems that were going to happen to Farouk just waited until Farida's divorce. It came from everywhere and from all directions. To list just a few of these problems Farouk had to face were:

- Labor and students began to demonstrate under the auspices of the high commissions of students and labor.
- The Abbas Bridge incident occurred when a major student protest turned violent and university students were killed in the process.
- The governor of Cairo governorate, Selim Pasha, was assassinated.
- Al Nokrashy and Ahmed Maher were assassinated.
- Some of the Egyptian judiciary and intelligence chiefs were assassinated.
- Farouk formed an "Iron Guard" to protect him, to spy on the army, and to even kill some of its undesirable leadership.
- He began to steer away from the spirit of the constitution and actually dissolved the popular Wafd majority government.
- There was the incident at Al-Kassassin where Farouk was involved in a car accident. This was also the beginning of Farouk's relationship with Nahed Rashad.
- There were the scandals that engulfed Princess Fawzyia, Farouk's sister, and the murder of Aly Ayoub's son in a sex-related incident. Aly Ayoub was the head of Al-Saady Party.
- There was the murder of Fahmy Abdelsalam Gomaa and the assassination of Amin Osman.
- There was the war in Palestine and the problem with the army's faulty weapons that killed many of those using them during the war.

- Cairo was burned on January 26, 1952, where Farouk was accused of involvement and conspiracy.
- Farouk's subsequently removed the popular Wafd cabinet for the second time.

It was the beginning of the end for Farouk and his rule of Egypt, where secret cells began to form in the army. The first indication that came on the public scene was when General Mohamed Nageib won the top post in the officer's club elections. This was followed by the army's revolution at midnight on July 23, 1952, the most serious and prominent event in the history of the Arab world and the Middle East throughout the twentieth century.

King Farouk was expelled into exile, and his son, Ahmed Fouad, heir to the throne, was installed in his place under the auspices of the Revolutionary Council.

On June 18, 1953, Egypt was proclaimed a republic, ending the royal dynasty of Mohamed Ali after one hundred and fifty years. That end came through the travesty of King Farouk's immaturity and poor judgment. It's a sad ending to what could have been and what might have been, but history does not forgive the fools who toy with their fate and the destiny of their people. The manner by which Farouk governed Egypt could not have produced other than what he got. Farouk messed up his golden opportunities for the thrills of his days.

The Queen Was the Leader of
Farouk's Opposition in the Palace

The queen continued her story while I sat with her in her small apartment in Maadi. As I looked at the queen's view of the beautiful flowers, it was as though these beautiful florets were looking at us from behind the glass window that reflected the glittering light rays from afar. It was a majestic view indeed. The queen was sitting quietly with deep sadness, telling volumes of how she felt inside.

She stopped momentarily and then said, "I was the only one who said no to Farouk, opposing many of his decisions and his actions. I revolted against his behavior. I did not do so for my sake or any personal reasons, but I did it to protect him and our lives as a family. It was for the sake of our daughters and, above all, the sake of our people, the Egyptian people, whom I loved dearly.

"No one else in the palace dared say no to Farouk, so they all banded together against me. Everyone acquiesced to Farouk's desires and demands, even those that were foolish and wrong. It all started with his Italian assistants and servants and then spread to the Egyptian employees in the palace. Even the politicians of the different parties parlayed around his wishes and gave him everything he wanted, even at the expense of his reputation or the interest of Egypt. I carried huge burdens inside me and tolerated everything Farouk did, hoping I would ultimately succeed in getting him to the right track and making him an honorable king for our people.

"It was too late to make changes in Farouk's personality, as he was spoiled and corrupted from a very young age. He was brought up in the wrong environment with the wrong mentors who appealed only to his desires as a young man. He was accustomed to having his wishes and orders implemented and followed, as he was the king. He was not used to having anyone objecting to his commands or offering him advice, so it always fell on deaf ears. No one around him in the palace cared for what was right or what was in the best interest of Egypt and the Egyptian people. They only cared about their own interests, which they got by delivering whatever Farouk wanted.

"If those around Farouk cared and provided him with the correct advice that would help the country, not themselves, things could have been different, and he would not have come to this tragic ending. Unfortunately, no one was listening, and I was like the romantic singer in a noisy hall full of loud music. No one could hear me. At times, I thought he was actually listening to me, but I quickly saw him doing the exact opposite of what I asked. He would only listen to his Italian servants, especially his personal assistant Pulli.

"Even his mother Nazly objected to his actions when they were contrary to her personal interests. It did not matter if these actions were in the best interest of the country or not or if they were in Farouk's own interest or not. Still, Farouk would not listen. After a while, Nazly too gave up and attended to her own special and personal interests, even at the expense of her son's reputation and good will. When the conflict between her and the king became so public, she actually left the country for a long time, a matter I would not want to get into here.

"As a matter of fact, a lot of people tried so hard to get me to stop my criticisms of Farouk. The common wisdom was that, for the sake of my daughters and myself, I should keep quite about what was happening at the palace. I could not, in all consciousness, do that and live with myself as an honorable and respected queen or even just as a mother. I remember that, among those who gave me lots of advice, was Prince Mohamed Ali, the elder of the royal family and the heir to the throne. Among them were also my mother and Queen Mother Nazly. In addition, the princesses and the princes, members of the cabinet, as well as many other close friends counseled me. I remember in particular Sir Miles Lampson, the representative of the British government, offering me advice, but I could not and would not listen. I insisted we all had to stand up to Farouk for the good of the country. I would do it all over again without any hesitation if that situation repeated itself today."

Nazly's Trickery

When we sat at the Diplomat Hotel in Bahrain, Farida told me about the tricks of Queen Mother Nazly, saying, "I remember when Queen Mother Nazly would send me gift packs, beautifully wrapped, but when I opened them, I would find dead frogs and slaughtered birds. I used to tolerate these silly pranks. There were so many of them that Nazly played against me to no end. Farouk would know about it, but he could not stand in the way of his mother. Nazly treated Farouk as the child she had, not as a responsible king, husband, and father.

"I knew that Nazly was interested in magic, a matter that frightened me. I tried to tell Farouk about it, but to no avail. He was in a different world by himself, uncaring and unconcerned with my fears. She was also a very aggressive and stubborn women. Farouk could not deal with that and said nothing about it, especially coming from his mother.

"I found myself alone in front of all these gangs. However, I was unyielding in the face of it all for eleven years. I had to give it all up for the sake of my sanity and my principles. There was nothing left for me to do but divorce and begin a new life for myself. I had to get back to my art and the passions I had, even before I married Farouk."

I asked the queen about Nazly's relationship with Ahmed Hussein. She told me, "I would rather not get into this. Their relationship was public and well known to everyone. It is a matter of public record, and I would rather not talk about it. However, I can tell you that Nazly and her stories were behind the downfall of Farouk and the revolution of 1952."

She went into silence, and I respected that and did not bring up the subject matter again. I knew that Farida knew the inside story of Queen Mother Nazly and Ahmed Hussein. While I also knew how much Farida suffered from Nazly and how her mother-in-law made her life like hell, Farida's pride and nobility would not allow her to delve into such personal matters of someone else. I knew that Ahmed Hussein failed Farouk at two important points in his life. The first was when he mentored him in England and used that as his entry into Egypt's governance. The second was when he established his elicit relationship with the queen mother.

Queen Mother Nazly and Her Daughters, the Princesses

"After King Fouad's death, it was as if Queen Mother Nazly had been born again. She began to enjoy her freedom and live a life of fun and joy. She began to mingle with everyone around her and actually had her civil marriage with Ahmed Hussein. She began to travel outside of Egypt and made every possible effort to enjoy her life. That did not sit well with Farouk, her son, now the king, and a great deal of disagreements began to surface and were known to everyone around her. At one point, Nazly went to Palestine, and while there, she was holding parties with the British officers at the famous King David Hotel. These parties brought anger and embarrassment to King Farouk. After the news of their parties became so widely known all over Egypt, Palestine, and Europe, the king sent his prime minister, Nahas Pasha, and his wife to Palestine to bring Nazly and her daughters back to Egypt.

"After the death of Ahmed Hussein, Nazly left Egypt for Europe and then went to the United States with the king's half-sisters, Princess Faika and Princess Fathia. What remained in the palace was a picture of Ahmed Hussein hanging on the wall crowned with a black ribbon. In the United States, a series of scandals began to surface about the relationships between the princesses and foreign service employees at the Egyptian Consulates. Of great embarrassment to King Farouk, in particular, was the reported relationship between Princess Fathia and Reyad Ghali, a Coptic employee at the Egyptian Foreign Ministry. Princess Fathia insisted on marrying Reyad Ghali at the strenuous objections of the king and his threats of boycotting her marriage and dishonoring her in Egypt.

"Nazly, for her part and to reduce the tensions, knowing Fathia's persistence on marrying Ghali, told Farouk that he would convert to Islam. It was a face-saving ploy for Farouk. Nazly also admonished him for objecting to actions that he allowed himself. That was followed with Princess Faika's marriage to Fouad Sadek, a consulate employee at the Egyptian Consulate in San Francisco. Over the king's objections, the marriages were consummated in civil ceremonies in the United State and then made legal under Islamic Sharia by Sheikh Al Azhar upon their return to Egypt.

"Once back in Egypt, the princesses joined in Farouk's own scandals, and the parties resumed from sundown to dawn where they all had their greatest fun and joy. There wasn't the slightest consideration of their official status as the royal family of Egypt. There was no consideration to the societal traditions or the country's religion. Nothing could stop such irresponsible acts, even when they were so much publicized in the media in Egypt, Europe, and the United States of America. This brought disgust and disdain among the Egyptian people who saw their traditions disgraced and their honor trampled into the ground by their irresponsible royalties.

"Princess Fawkia, Farouk's half-sister, was not party to much of what was going on at the time. She lived a low-key life and married the Egyptian ambassador to France, Mr. Mahmoud Fakhry. She did not have much of a relationship with Farouk. On the other hand, Princess Faiza, Farouk's other sister, married Mohamed Ali Raouf, the grandson of Princess Fatima Ismail, in 1945. Princess Faiza also had her own share of scandals and rumors, being so beautiful and much involved in the social affairs of many charitable organizations. The nonstop partying with the diplomatic corps kept her in the public eye, which helped spread rumors about here with ease.

"The night of July 23, 1952, the night of the revolution, the princess was dancing with the secretary of the American Embassy at the Romance nightclub in Alexandria until the wee hours of the morning.

"The closest of the sisters to Farouk was Princess Fawzyia, who was married to the Shah of Iran. Princess Fawzyia later married

Ismail Sherine, who became the minister of defense toward the end of Farouk's reign.

"That was how Farouk's family lived. Their family relationships were so torn and complicated, full of disagreements and controversy. There was no kinship among the family members and no intimacy, as would be expected in a Muslim family governed by the known Egyptian and Islamic traditions. That was not to be, and it was clear to the Egyptian people, much to their chagrin, that the royal family was not conducting itself as a dignified ruling royal family. This may have advanced the timing of the revolution and made it so much easier to accept by the people who had already lost their faith in the royal family and the king. The revolution took place without a single shot with the ultimate termination of the Mohamed Ali dynasty in Egypt.

"And so ended the scandals and moral corruption in the palace that were the mainstay of the royal family life and traditions. As angry as the people were, the simple Arabic proverb that became popular at that time was 'That who cannot control his mother cannot govern a nation,' so befitting to Farouk's dilemma.

"After Farouk's exile, Nazly and her daughter Fathia and her husband Reyad Ghali left for Europe and then went to the United States, carrying with them what they could of money and jewelry. In the United States, they continued to live the high life, spending all they could as if there were no end to their fortunes. Not accustomed to managing their finances, they spent their fortune and had to face their expected ends. When their money and jewelry were gone, there followed the divorce between Fathia and Reyad Ghali, who by that time had three children, two boys and a girl.

Reyad Ghali and Princess Fathia at
their marriage ceremony in the USA.

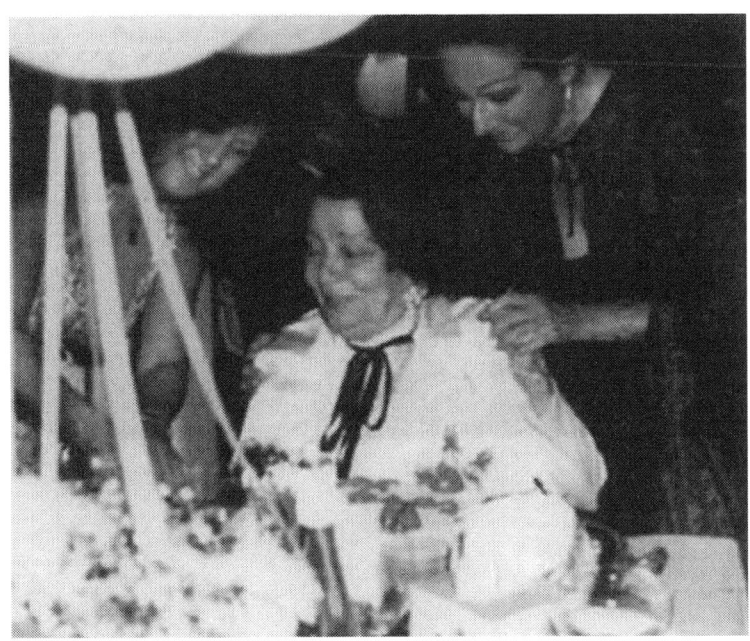

Princess Fathia celebrating her mothers' birthday, Queen
Mother Nazly, before Princes Fathia was killed by her
husband Reyad Ghali, in Lose Angeles . . .

"Unable to live the life of poverty, Fathia decided to return to Egypt. However, when Reyad Ghali learned of that, he asked to see her for the last time before she left for Egypt. Against the advice and insistence of her children not to go to that meeting, Fathia went to see her former husband for the last time, and there he shot her six times, killing her instantly. That was the end of Princess Fathia's life in the United States on December 10, 1976. Reyad Ghali was arrested and tried on first-degree murder. His trial in Los Angeles, California, ended two years later with a life sentence on May 2, 1978. Ghali, however, was not to survive his sentence and died, supposedly by committing suicide in prison, on August 25 of the same year.

"Queen Mother Nazly, to whom people attributed all those royal family misfortunes, also met her unfortunate end in the United States. In the process, she lost her royal titles by Farouk's decree on August 8, 1950. Nazly died in poverty in Los Angeles on May 29, 1978. She was buried next to her daughter Fathia, ending the royal family's chapter in the United States. There remains the Ghali children, who continued their residence in the United States since."

Queen Farida and the Crown

For eleven years, Queen Farida held the royal crown of Egypt. When she asked for her divorce from King Farouk, she had no hesitation, not even for a second, knowing full well she was throwing it all away. As we sat at the dinner table at the famous and historical George V Hotel in Paris, I asked Queen Farida how it felt living at the palace as the queen of Egypt, wearing that royal crown.

Without hesitation, Farida quickly responded, "I lived in that palace for eleven years as the queen, but in name only. I was like a prisoner in that palace living a strange life, lonely in the midst of all the servants and associates who cared for all my needs and more. I did not feel their presence, as they were foreign to me, unaware of what was going on deep in my heart. I had no one to express my feelings to, no one to talk to who had any understanding of what I was going through and the trauma I was experiencing. They were all strangers to me. I could not put my trust into anyone and tell him or her about my emotional ambivalence even when everyone was trying to comfort me. I did not even feel safe among them.

"That was not what I envisioned my life would be like with Farouk. He had his mother live with us at the palace, meddling into everything I needed to do for my husband and my children. She would get into the most intimate details of our private life. Contrary to what I thought her presence with us would do, I hoped she would provide her wisdom and experience to me. Beginning my married life with her son Farouk, I thought she would be the person with whom I could express my difficulties and who could help me fit into this new life, the life of the royal palace. I was not accustomed to palace life before, so having someone who could help me deal with the servants and assistants would have been an enormous advantage for me, as they gave me no privacy whatsoever.

"To tell you the truth, I must say I enjoyed the queen mother's presence with us at the beginning, and I was initially comfortable with her taking part in our life for all the reasons I just mentioned. At times, she stood by me and protected me, offering her experience in dealing with matters I was not used to. However, that comfort did not last for long, and my life began to unravel in a manner I could not have imagined. Not only that, but the queen mother actually began to work against me and take every opportunity to complain about me to her son. There was no mercy in how we could deal with one another. War started between Nazly and me, and there was no chance that I could save my daughters and my husband from her vicious manipulations that ensued. It was hell. I can actually still feel the misery I had, living and tasting the bitter poison I was receiving every day from Nazly. I was the queen in name, but I was, in reality, a prisoner of my circumstances.

"The worst of the worse surrounded Farouk. Women were constantly paraded around him, satisfying his desires. He was the king, and all else were there to serve his needs any way they could. I used to look for my husband everywhere, but he was nowhere to be found. Eventually, I would learn that he was gone with his friends, his hypocritical companions, to the nightclubs to drink and gamble all night.

"You can imagine how I felt when his daughters, the princesses, asked me, 'Where is our father?' and I had no answer. I can imagine the pictures of the women whom he kept, the lovers he partied the nights with, while I was home and could not even close my eyes to sleep. I was tormented with a constant struggle inside me, as I wanted so much to hold on to him and save my marriage for the sake of the children.

Queen Farida with her three daughters, Feryal, Fawzyia and Fadia.at the Abdeen Palace, before she asked for her divorce.from King Farouk.

After all, he was the father of my daughters, and with me, he would be saved from all the ills that were consuming his life."

The queen continued, in remembrance of her years at the palace with Farouk, the times where she should have had the real life of a queen in love with her prince, the king of Egypt, "I was seventeen years old when I married Farouk. At that time, Queen Mother Nazly was forty, emboldened by her years of experience and the longtime residence with the palace servants and assistants, both inside and outside the palace. She was also a friend of my mother's. After our marriage, I began to see the differences in our personalities, in how we viewed things and lived our lives. I was the quiet, tender person. I loved my family life with my husband and children, going to bed early and all. Nazly, on the other hand, was an outgoing, party-loving person, much like her son Farouk. I guess that was where he obviously got his bad habits from, the ones that eventually cost him his throne. I thought the palace would have a special management group that would take care of the formal royal events and celebrations. A special group would take care of meeting and greeting the many dignitaries that came to the palace on many occasions. As it turned out, none of that existed, and Nazly fit very well with that aspect of the palace life. It matched her personality to the T and helped make for the loud and noisy parties at the palace, not only for the official occasions but also for her friends and acquaintances.

"Nazly did not like my attitude and objections to a lot of what she was doing. Our friendship quickly evaporated. Nazly became angry with me, and from that point, she declared war. She made every effort to bring everyone to her side, especially Farouk, against my daughters and me. She began to spread rumors about me. She'd send her emissaries to tell me that Farouk was with this woman or that, just to make me angry and to get me to make mistakes that in turn got Farouk mad at me as well. She was the source of the many false tales that used to spread through the palace like fire, so quickly and so determinedly.

"One time when Prince Mohamed Ali came to my father's house after I left the palace, to try to convince me to go back and to mend my relationship with Farouk, he said, 'I know Nazly is behind all these actions that happened to you. I am afraid it will also happen to Farouk.' Sure enough, that was what happened soon thereafter when Farouk lost everything and ended the dynasty started by his great-great grandfather almost one hundred and fifty years ago.

"The strange thing was that Farouk was very weak in his relationship with his mother. Her desires and demands superseded everything. On the night of our wedding and in response to one of her demands, Farouk signed a proclamation, which said,

In my name, Farouk the First, King of Egypt, hereby proclaim, in view of our esteemed love and admiration for the Queen Mother, our dearest mother, and for her greatness and for giving her great name to this great kingdom of ours, and to commemorate her life at the highest order, we have therefore ordered the following:

1. *That the title of the Royal Queen Mother, our dearest mother, henceforth shall be Her Royal Highness Queen Nazly and*

2. *That the prime minister and our chief of staff shall execute our order, heretofore proclaimed at Kobba Palace on the 18th of January 1938.*

Signed,

Farouk

This proclamation given on the eve of Farida's wedding was a clear signal of what was to come after that between Nazly and Farida. Both were queens, but who would have the authority, and who would be in name only? It was clearly a recipe for all the infighting that took over the palace thereafter.

"I Was the Source of Happiness in My Family"

"I lived in Alexandria, the pride jewel of the Mediterranean. I lived there since I was a child and through my youth until I was engaged to Farouk. The beautiful blue water of the Mediterranean, the sea waves, and the flocks of seagulls were my greatest inspiration. I was always a source of happiness for my family, even when I was a child. I was a quiet child growing up and at peace with herself. My interactions with others and responses to events around me were tempered and polite. I lived a simple life. I loved to read and listen to music, especially classical music. I never tired of listening to music, as music soothed my feelings toward all around me.

"During my childhood and early teens, my life was simple. People who loved each other and me surrounded me. It was an environment where kindness was the predominant character of the whole family. There were no quarrels and no fighting amongst us. We went through our days with love and joy. There was no care other than loving one another and seeking happiness amongst ourselves.

Queen Farida's family, her father Youssef Zul-Faquar and her
mother Zaineb Hanem and her two brothers Said and Sherif.

"It was the simple life of a young girl living in the midst of
her family, a father who was a judge at the Alexandria High Court
and a mother who befriended most of the Egyptian society women
and was a close friend of Queen Nazly, King Farouk's mother. And
after my marriage to King Farouk, I was also the source of joy
and happiness to my family. My father, Judge Youssef Zul-Faquar,
was named Pasha, and my mother was awarded Weshah El Neel,
the Nile's highest honor. I was happy for the proclamations and
acknowledgements to my family by the king, as I loved them so much

and had all the affection and respect for them. My father raised me in the best form with respect for justice closely tied to my soul. I was also happy for my mother who was the friend of Nazly and the one who insisted, with my father's approval, that I accompany Farouk to Europe in 1937, where our love was born. That European trip, in fact, led to our marriage. My mother was actually the first associate of the queen mother, and their close friendship brought both great joy and sorrow into my life.

"Unfortunately, I was also the cause of their sadness when they began to witness and live through my marriage difficulties and the troubles that Farouk and I had just one year after our marriage. I barely had one year of a happy married life with Farouk before our troubles began to surface and our differences came to be recognized by all around us inside and outside the palace, including my family.

"In the first couple of years, I tried to hide my emotions and show a good face in front of everyone in the palace, except I could not hide my troubles from my family. I tried hard to deal with all the new elements that suddenly began to crop up in front of me. I had to deal with them with the demeanor of a strong person, but to no avail. It eventually became too much for me to bear.

"The palace environment was not the kind of setting to raise children, especially among the servants and associates who knew nothing about morality, decency, or respect for privacy. I began to build my own cocoon to shelter my daughters and myself from all that was happening around us in the palace. I did not want to raise them as Farouk was, spoiled and selfish. I established my own upbringing style and behaved like the cat that hugged her kittens to protect them. I wanted to keep them safe from all the predators around us, especially in that complex environment of the royal palace."

Farida's family life was in stark contrast to that of the palace. It was the life of a loving and well-mannered family that held to the highest of ethical standards. After all, she was the daughter of an eminent justice of the International Appeals Court. He was also the son of Aly Pasha Zul-Faquar, the former governor of Cairo, who was the son of Youssef Beck Rasmi, one of the leaders of the Egyptian Army at the time of Khedevie Ismail. On her mother's side was Mrs. Zeinab Zul-Faquar, the daughter of the late Mohamed Said Pasha, who was asked to head the Egyptian Cabinet more than once. Queen Farida also had two brothers, Said and Sherif Zul-Faquar.

Farida's real name was Safinaz. She attended Notre Dame De Scion, the French high school in Alexandria. She learned English and French in addition to Arabic, of course. Actually, her father would get her special tutors for Arabic and Islamic teaching to make sure she was well versed in both for herself and her family.

Farida had many hobbies. Music was her primary delight, especially playing the piano. Her father, Youssef Pasha, was not only an excellent pianist but also a great painter. No wonder she too became an artist of her own, taking after her father and uncle. One could see his great oil painting on the wall at the palace entrance, a testament to his talent as a great artist.

Queen Farida was particularly fond of classical music. She had her own collection of the best of the best in classical music.

"Music and art are so much intertwined in my life. When I tire of one, I automatically go to the other; they were my relief from the activities around me at the palace. They gave me comfort, especially when Farouk used to go out all night with his Italian friends." After a short pause, Queen Farida continued, "Now, music and art are what is left in my life. I live with my art and my music. They bring back some of my old happy memories, even if it were for a moment or two. They provide me emotional peace and security against any difficulty that I face. They save me from going insane."

The Sad Smile: Queen Farida and Her Political Views

Queen Farida's quite smile clearly showed her sadness more than her joy. Anyone could see that. She was a great reader and a fantastic listener as well. She followed international affairs with great enthusiasm and devotion. She had strong opinions about what was going on outside Egypt's borders. She also had her own opinions about the political affairs of the country. She voiced her opinions on matters of public interest with care and sensitivity. She did that as a private citizen, not as a queen, so she would not influence the public discourse in the country. That was the case both under the rule of Farouk when Egypt was a monarchy and continued after Egypt became a republic after Farouk's exile.

The queen said, "It saddens me to see the affairs of today's political parties. These parties are not working with any program or vision that can move the country forward. That used to be the case during Farouk's reign. The Egyptian political parties, like Al Wafd under Nahas Pasha, were strong and had influence on how the monarchy was ruled, even under British occupation."

The queen liked to be with the people and found comfort in being with the villagers and farmers. She loved the country life in the villages where there was so much kindness. It was much more than when she interacted with those who had the titles and fortunes in the cities and among the elites.

She was a queen who felt that, if Farouk had lived the life she wanted for him and her family, the life of honesty and discipline, he might not have lost his throne. Farouk was a kind and loving man. "He had the love and respect of his people and the respect of the Egyptian Army. He learned the teachings of Islam, and he was as pure as anyone could be, extending his authority from Al Azhar, the highest religious authority in the country. He was also convinced of the importance of Egypt to the Arab world, and he had great influence, internally and externally on the international stage."

"These abilities were clearly evident at the time of his coronation and when we got married, except for the early influence of Ahmed Hussein who mentored Farouk in England before King Fouad's death. Farouk was otherwise well groomed for the role of the leader not only of Egypt but also of the Arab world. He could have become just that, as he had no competition that could stand in his way. He could have even been the leader of the Islamic world if he wanted to. Among his great supporters in this was Imam Al Maraghy, Sheikh Al Azhar. That relationship, however, worked against him from the perspectives of the British authorities and the Egyptian political parties. In those days, Farouk had the final say in all matters, deriving his power from the support of the people and the army."

The queen paused for a moment. "But after my divorce, the palace became unruly, and the king began to lose his political support from the people and the army. The army that protected him in his initial days in power was changing. Control of the palace affairs changed hands to Farouk's servants and associates who had no interest in the well-being of the country or Farouk himself.

"You see, Farouk delegated his authority to his clan and the palace cronies, those who attended to his lust and around-the-clock partying. They were a combination of foreign surrogates and/or a group of disinterested and incompetent Egyptian personnel. At one point and for a period of time, this group had full control over Egypt. You could imagine the fate of Egypt in the hands of incompetents. The country with the greatest civilization since Cleopatra and Ramses and the country with influence on the world stage, politically, economically, and socially, became controlled by the likes of Farouk's court, who had no interest but their own wealth and survival.

"With that, Egypt became vulnerable to deceit and trickery, a magnet for corruption and intrigue. The forces that used to protect the king against the British Embassy were now in control and worked against the palace and Farouk. Even his Islamic supporters embodied in the persona of Sheikh Al Azhar disbanded, leaving Farouk totally alone and vulnerable to the takeover, which eventually took place on July 23, 1952.

"As soon as Farouk gave up the reins of power to this gang of Italian and Egyptian servants, he had already lost the battle. The royal activities and proclamations and much of the country's business began to run down from neglect. Farouk did not even have the time to sign his own proclamations. The writing was already on the wall. Farouk's days were numbered. People's prayers and the Duaa that was usually offered to the king during mosque's sermons at the Gomaa Prayers were no longer given. In fact, public incrimination of the king and the palace were now the common messages given at the mosques. The protection that used to come from the religious community was no longer there. Al Azhar's unconditional support vanished and was replaced by attacks on the king and the palace alike.

"With the death of Al Maraghy, Al Azhar quickly turned against Farouk, and Farouk lost a very important pillar in his support base. Once that support evaporated, Farouk's opposition mounted in public. The rumors and scandals about what was happening at the palace openly became the talk of the town, the press, and the foreign diplomatic corps as well. This opposition was not only against Farouk but also against his palace associates, the 'corrupt gang,' as they were referred to.

"All this deterioration had great influence on people's anger and public dissent. After the tragic Cairo fires of January 26, 1952, Cairo began to be blanketed with an eerie and deafening quiet, the one that usually comes before the storm that was about to happen. The July 23 officer's revolution was the storm that was about to happen, and Farouk finally met his unfortunate destiny and expulsion from Egypt. He was removed altogether from the throne and exiled to Italy, the country of his choosing.

"Farouk thought the army that was his last armor, would come to his defense, but they came this time to exile him out of Egypt. When I used to criticize him for his ill treatment of people, Farouk used to say, 'The army is my army, and its men are my best armor. They all love me and are loyal to my throne.' He had forgotten that the army men were plotting to overthrow him with their own revolution.

"Farouk tried during his last days in power to hold on to his throne and to begin to pay attention to his rule again, but it was too late. His supporting institutions had already crumbled; his public support and love from the Egyptian people had also run down to its lowest levels. His latest attempts for his own rescue were apparent as he was constantly changing the cabinet in the last months and days before his exile. The time had already passed, and it was inevitable that his rule would end the way it did. In fact, he tried to pass on his throne to his son Ahmed Fouad, who was only two years old at the time, but there was no throne to heir, only a remnant of a destroyed dynasty that he was trying to hand down and keep going on through his infant son.

"I will never forget that moment, the one when Farouk relinquished his throne and left Egypt. I sat down in my pyramid's palace balcony, listening to the radio, gazing into history, looking at the Giza Pyramids and the Sphinx in front of me, reflecting on the ages that passed by since the times of the Pharos, and recognizing that nothing is eternal. People, thrones, and dynasties, all are finite, and nothing is forever except God the Almighty. So will Egypt and the Nile, they will be there after all else had gone except for the crown of love.

"I ran to the streets and quickly went into a nearby bookstore and bought a French book about the French Revolution. I also picked up a few paintbrushes and a few color tubes. I said to myself at that moment, 'Today, I'll begin a new life. This time, it will be a life with art.' Tears ran down my cheeks as I looked around myself, watching groups of people happily parading and celebrating the events of the day. The revolution started, and people were chanting that God had finally avenged them. My tears were not for a passing dynasty or a lost crown. My tears were for my daughters who left with Farouk on that yacht, *Al Mahrousa*, without me having a chance to say good-bye. I went back to begin a new life with art."

Princess Feryal's Message to Queen Farida before Her Departure

"When I knew that Farouk was leaving the country on board of *Al Mahrousa* and he was taking my daughters with him without my having had a chance to see them, I cried and could not stop my tears from running down my cheeks. I did not know when I would see them again. As I learned later, Farouk had relinquished his throne and signed a decree that he would have to leave before six o'clock that evening. The day was Sunday, July 26, 1952. Farouk did not tell me what was happening or the timeline he had to abide by. I did not know that he was also taking our daughters with him. After their departure, I received a message from my older daughter Feryal, in which she wrote:

My Dear Mother, I have to leave without saying good-bye to you. I used to wait for Fridays of every week to see you. Now there will be many Fridays without my kissing you! Please forgive me, Mother, as I was not always the obedient daughter. I may have made mistakes unintentionally; I may have caused you pain without knowing that I did. But I love you, and forgive me for not being able to kiss you good-bye, as my father did not permit me to do so. Signed, Feryal

"King Farouk was in a very nervous state as he tried to hold on to his emotions in front of his family, his servants, and associates. When Soliman Hafez came carrying the document relinquishing his right to the throne, Farouk tried to add a few comments to it, but Soliman Hafez explained that it was beyond his role as a messenger, he came only to carry the document in its final form, and no one had the authority to change it. The document was formulated as a royal decree, giving up the rights to the throne.

"What might have shown the emotional state that Farouk came into that day and the enormous anger inside him was that his first signature was so erratic from his wobbly hands that he decided to sign another copy. As he was signing the second document, he told Soliman Hafez, 'You may understand the situation and forgive me that my signature was not the way I would like it to be, so I'll sign another one.' And so, he did sign another document for the record books.

"Another event that happened on that last day, Farouk asked to have his lunch at the royal dining room, where he met with his sisters, Fawzyia and Faiza, and Faiza's husband. The Revolutionary Council had agreed that King Farouk would sail on the royal yacht, *Al Mahrousa*, and Farouk stood there at the dock, wearing his uniform as the commander-in-chief of the royal navy. As he stood there talking to Aly Maher Pasha, he said, 'It is getting late, and I have to get to *Al Mahrousa*.' He climbed into the boat that would take him to the yacht. Aly Maher Pasha could not hold himself and cried as he saw that ending to the young king.

"Ali Maher remembered that, at that same dock some fifteen years earlier, he welcomed young Farouk when he came back from England after his father's death. At that time, Farouk was coming to take over his father's throne. After Farouk went on board *Al Mahrousa*, General Mohamed Naguib, the head of the Revolutionary Council, came on board at six o'clock with two members of the revolutionary council, Air Force Lieutenant General Gamal Salem and Lieutenant General Hussein El Shafie, accompanying him to see the king off and give the proper military salute to King Farouk.

A rare photo of the Egyptian Revolutionary
Council with all of its members, in 1952.

"*Al Mahrousa* was to return to Alexandria immediately after King Farouk disembarked in Italy. These were the orders given to the yacht captain, Captain Galal Allouba. It is ironic that this same yacht, *Al Mahrousa*, was the ship that took Khedevie Ismail to Italy, also after the British exiled him many decades earlier.

"In 1976, I had the opportunity to have lunch on board of this yacht during the Bicentennial Flagship Celebration in New York. *Al Mahrousa* was among the participating Egyptian ships and came all the way from Alexandria. It was one of the elite Navy ships that came representing the many participating nations. I clearly remember the beautiful ornaments, as the ship was decorated with gold handles. It was a magnificently decorated yacht and one of the most beautiful and powerful yachts in the world. It was a historical treasure, dating back to the early years of the Mohamed Aly dynasty that ruled Egypt for over a hundred and fifty years. *Al Mahrousa* was refurbished and retooled several times, and it kept its international stature and historical value. The American Navy brass admired it enormously. Even as a yacht, it was equipped with a powerful engine that could run as a big ship."

Accompanying the king to Italy was his family, which was made up of Queen Nariman, his second wife who gave him an heir to the throne, Ahmed Fouad, and his three daughters from Queen Farida, Feryal, Fawzyia, and Fadia. He also took with him one hundred and fifty suitcases and steamer trunks carrying his personal belongings. After everyone was on board *Al Mahrousa*, the farewell ceremony was conducted, and the royal flag was taken down. The Egyptian national anthem was played, and the officer who took down the flag folded it and kissed it before handing it over to the king.

In accordance with the traditional military procedure, a twenty-one gun salute was also fired while the honor guard stood in attention, giving their final military salute to the retired king. That was how the Mohamed Ali dynasty ended after ruling Egypt from 1805 to 1952.

When the Queen and the Chauffer Cried

"After marrying Farouk, I lived in huge palaces, but with all the space I had, I used to feel imprisoned. After my divorce, I moved to the Pyramid's Palace where I lived for a while until the revolutionary government took it away from me and confiscated it. My life began to take a downturn to the worst it had been. I had no place to stay. I used to move from one friend's or relative's house to another, so I always felt tightness in my chest, almost unable to breathe, always looking for some space where I could breathe and feel the air around me."

Queen Farida's three-room apartment in Maadi was so small that one could not move in it with ease. One had to be careful walking around for fear of breaking something. That was how small it was. This tightness in space caused her enormous emotional anguish as well and made her nerves very sensitive to anything that happened around her. She used to go to Al-Mokattam, a high hill on the east side of Cairo, where she could have some air to breathe and relieve her nerves. She would go there three or four times a week to look at Cairo under this thick layer of grayish-yellow cloud of polluted air. That was, in fact, where people in Cairo were living, breathing, and carrying on their daily lives.

At one point, Queen Farida told me, as she laughed with sadness in her voice, Al-Mokattam, was the spacious apartment she had. After she lost her apartment on the Nile, the one President Sadat promised her, she made Al-Mokattam her daily escape to which she would go as frequently as she could. On a clear day, she could see the pyramids from her seat at Al-Mokattam. Looking at the stars at night under the moonlight, Farida watched the panoramic view of Cairo.

"I felt peace throughout my body and my soul. Then I went back to my small apartment in Maadi to sleep. The next dawn, I started my day again."

One day, I sent my driver to Queen Farida to pick her up for an event we hosted for her. On the way back, the driver would close the car windows, so as not to disturb her hair from the wind. She would quickly tell him, "Open all the windows. I want to breathe this air. Isn't it enough that I am missing this in my apartment? It is like a matchbox." The driver cried in disbelief. He could not imagine that the former queen of Egypt would be living in such a small apartment, like his own. What was worse was that the government gave this apartment to the former queen while he inherited his apartment from his family.

The queen cried for the driver's tears. No one knew that her pride would have prevented her from crying, but the tears just kept running down endlessly.

Queen Farida in her Apartment in Maadi.

My driver, Hussein, came to ask me, "Is this true? The queen is living in such a small apartment."

I answered, "Yes, Hussein, and her mother shares it with her as well. She has no place to paint or to do her work, so she converted her kitchen into a gallery using mirrors to make it look bigger and more spacious!"

One time, Queen Farida and I were walking the beautiful streets in Bahrain when we stood watching the construction of a bridge that connected Bahrain with Saudi Arabia. Farida said, "See how clean the air is here. I hate the small and crowded places. These dirty and dusty places are so unnerving to me. I cannot imagine how people in

Cairo leave the garbage mount in front of their homes the way they do and not feel crowded or shamed. These places kill me. I always get shocked just looking at them. That is why I look for space, clean air, and clean water wherever I go."

We stood there quietly for a while, looking at the skies and the glitter of lights against the ocean waves, listening to the sound of those waves rushing to the shore. We saw the beautiful green trees and the artistic statues as a testament of Bahraini's love and respect for beauty and art. The whole place was like a huge park with beautiful trees, flowers, and roses of all kinds, beautifully spaced out over the landscape, like a great symphony playing to the Almighty God, the creator of all things.

In the midst of all this serenity and beauty, where the queen was happily enjoying a light breeze of fresh air, she told me, "You know, I had hard times in my life, but did you know that at times I had to sell some of my gifts that were given to me to live on? I was so ashamed to do that myself, so I always had others do it for me. I did not want people to know that my life had become so difficult or that I could not provide for my own sustenance. I sold my silver platters and my arts and crafts just to survive."

The Queen and Egypt's Presidents

"The July 23 revolution was not a surprise to me, as I had predicted it before it actually happened. In fact, I told Farouk over and over again before our divorce, 'The Egyptian people and the army loved you and were loyal to you during the early years of your rule. They supported you in every way against the British and the political parties. They shall abandon you as you abandoned them. You'll lose the support of all around you, those who supported you, including your wife and daughters. They shall not hold on or be patient forever.'

"I did not say these words to caution him against what was coming, as I had given up trying to correct his behavior, but it was my last advice to Farouk before our divorce. I had my own reasons, however, namely that there were people in the palace who were not corrupted and who cared for the well-being of the country. They used to tell me things that Farouk did not know or hear about. I was also able to see beyond what was happening, as though looking from the outside in, something Farouk was too preoccupied to notice. I was able to reach the many truths that were not on Farouk's mind

"Farouk became annoyed with himself and all those who continued to give him advice warning him that he was getting too close to the brink, especially me. Many a time, he would tell me, 'Listen, my father is dead, and he was the only one I could listen to, and you are not my father.'

"After the revolution, the country and the people honored me and gave me a title that I'll always cherish over all else, 'Farida, The Love of the People.' I regained my freedom and mobility after I used to be followed by an entourage of secret servicemen recording every move I made and following me everywhere I went, even after my divorce. I used to limit my movement following their recommendations that I would not be safe going here or there to the point I was worried that they would in fact do what they warned me of.

"With the revolution, a huge burden of fear was removed off my chest. People began to express their feelings freely to me. Their love was expressed wherever I was, even in the streets. An expression of that love was when *Al Mouswar* magazine put my picture on the magazine cover only weeks after the revolution in August 1952, I think. The magazine named me the 'People's Love,' and that was my best title ever and even more precious than the royal crown itself or any other crown."

The queen laughed. "I actually regained the title of the queen even after the government banned the titles and the monarchy had fallen. Although the Revolutionary Council confiscated my palace, which Farouk gave to me as a gift, they did not deny me any of my requests."

The Queen and President Nasser

"A few years after the '52 revolution, I requested permission to travel to Beirut, Lebanon. My request was granted without exception. When President Nasser heard of my request, he said 'Why are you keeping her here in Egypt? She can travel at any time to anywhere she wants.' So I went to Beirut in 1963. At that time, travel visas were not easily granted, and Nasser's decision was quite open-ended, allowing me to travel to Beirut and stay as long as I wanted.

Beirut, the Heavens and Hell

"I said good-bye to my friends and relatives in Cairo. Good-bye to the Capital of the Nile. Good-bye to the kind hearts and the simple people who covered me with their love and deep affection. They were the ones who crowned me with the Love Crown. I said good-bye to all that and left for Beirut."

"That was in 1963, eleven years after the Egyptian Revolution of 1952. In Beirut, I tried to put the past behind me with all of its pain and anxiety; to discover the future and live a new life in this magical city, the one that is famous for its glamour and different from all other capitals in the world. Beirut is unique for its special beauty and wonderful blend of lifestyles, those of the East and the West mixed in one place and one tradition."

Queen Farida chose Lebanon to be one of her preferred spots to live and hoped that Beirut would be a beautiful sanctuary for her, a place where she could have a restful life and, at the same time, enjoy the serenity and quiet beauty of the city. It was a new beginning for Queen Farida, away from the tug of war that characterized her life experience in Egypt. Moving to Beirut was getting away from the political upheavals and constant struggle for power that was the nature of beast in the palace life in Egypt.

It was not an easy decision to make, as she had to get the approval of President Nasser to leave the country, so it was a mixed blessing to get his approval and to travel to Beirut. However, with all the anticipation Queen Farida had for her new life and the great expectations, just leaving Cairo for Beirut was not easy to get out from under the cloud of sadness that had characterized her life with Farouk. She returned to her original passion, painting, and began to bury her emotions into her paintings in every which way she could.

She would paint and paint and invite her friends and acquaintances whenever she had an opportunity for that. "They liked my paintings. They encouraged me to continue to paint and expand my painting landscape into new horizons. That helped my work enormously, and my paintings began to evolve in many directions. The empty canvases now began to grow into landscapes of light, color, and shadows.

"Beirut was my sanctuary from what I had been through. Many of my friends and associates helped me, and they were generous with me at every corner I turned to. However, my life in Beirut was not uneventful. Living in a city well known for its excitement and joyful atmosphere was great fun for me. I also liked the quiet life and adored the time I spent with my brushes and in front of my canvases.

Queen Farida with Mrs. Soad Hamdy, in Beirut, after an evening party.

"Nevertheless, I could not get rid of the sadness inside me, even with my friends who surrounded me with their love and care. I tried to avoid problems and just simply look the other way, but I could not. I was haunted with my memories that would not leave me alone. I was alone even when I had everyone around me.

"The truth is that I eventually started to breathe in Beirut. I began to feel safe and restful, and I had a chance to look back at my life and make every effort to turn that page into a hopeful future. Living in Beirut to me was like living in a mixture of heavens and hell, like experiencing a life in paradise while being tortured all in one. You cannot imagine the extent of torture that I was living through."

Those were Farida's own words, and just seeing and hearing her describe her life and watch her emotions as she described what she had been through in each phase of her life could not be articulated in words.

"I had a beautiful and spacious apartment in Beirut in one of the most beautiful suburbs, the well-known city of Rosha. I lived in the famous Al Than apartment building. My apartment overlooked the Mediterranean Sea, and I had one of the most beautiful views that God created. This great suburb and the view of the beautiful blue water, as far as the eye could see, gave me eternal peace and brushed away some of my sadness. I reconnected with my friends and acquaintances, old and new. I got my own car and driver waiting for anything I wanted to do. It was just great. I was invited to lots of parties and events, some I accepted and others I declined. I had many visitors who kept me company. It was the overall atmosphere—the nightlife of Beirut with its clubs and great restaurants, the social life with the people, and their joyful outlook for life. It was just a great new life for me."

"In Beirut, I Thought of Committing Suicide"

The Lebanese people, with their different political affiliations, religions, economic levels, and even ideologies, all shared one thing and one thing only. They were insatiably in love with freedom. I got to know many people, friends, relatives, and even acquaintances I had known during my life in royalty with Farouk. A great many people wanted to know me. I even had marriage proposals from many, but I was torn inside and did not know where I was going. I was afraid of what the future would bring. I began to feel that my life could not continue like that. I began to face many unwelcomed approaches from people I did not even know. People wanted to befriend me even when I did not want to know them.

"This change in my life, even after a short while in Beirut, began to close in on me and destroy my sense of peace. While I was hoping to settle there for a long time, it was not to be. This would be the first time where I had a chance to live a life of joy and happiness in a city and among people who loved life and fun, but it was cut short. I began to go back into seclusion. I was not interested in being with people, the same ones with whom I had great times at first when I arrived in Beirut. The change was difficult for me and brought me back to my memories when Farouk and I were separated. Two choices faced me, neither of which was pleasant, either go crazy or commit suicide.

"My life in Beirut was very different from that in Cairo. What added more to my difficulties in Beirut were the many offers of marriage, which I got from kings and prime ministers. I even got an offer from one of the royal sheikhs of one of the Arab countries, and please do not ask me who. I decided to stay away from all people and go back and put my faith in God the Almighty. He is the savior of those who were in trouble. God protected me. From that moment, God became my sanctuary, living with me in my blood and in my soul. My soul could no longer be separated from my body.

"These difficult moments culminated into my decision to travel to Saudi Arabia to do Umrah. I wanted to wash away my sorrow and escape the marriage proposals and all that was haunting me in Beirut. It was not a hasty decision on my part but a deliberate one. I simply needed to do it for my own sanity.

"I still remember that morning when I was sitting in my balcony in Beirut, and all of a sudden, I got up, went to my car, and asked my driver to take me to the Saudi Embassy. The ambassador greeted me warmly, and I told him of my desire to get his permission to travel to Saudi Arabia to perform Umrah. I asked him to let the king's wife, Queen Effat, know of my wish. I wanted to be close to God and to bring back my peace of mind. A few days later, the ambassador contacted me, having taken care of all the arrangements on my behalf for my visit. He informed me of the queen's gratitude and her welcoming my visit to Mecca. I packed my bags and left Beirut."

The News of Farouk's Death

"I was in Beirut when I learned of Farouk's passing in Italy in 1965. As soon as I heard the news, I immediately contacted Cairo and kept in constant communication with the authorities, day and night, requesting permission for Farouk's burial in Cairo. When President Nasser learned about that and my wish to have Farouk's body brought to Egypt for burial, he agreed and actually sent a private plane to bring the body from Rome to Cairo. I flew to Rome immediately, and from there, we boarded the plane with Farouk's body to Cairo. On the plane were our daughters, his sisters, and Prince Ahmed Fouad, Farouk's son from Nariman, and me. The plane landed at midnight on March 27, 1965, and Farouk was buried before dawn that same night. There were no ceremonies or even the presence of anyone other than the immediate family. These were the conditions for allowing his burial in Egypt altogether. We implemented these conditions to the letter.

"That night, a new dawn started for me, one that began to take shape in the night's sky as I found myself crying alone for Farouk's passing. I remembered the few good memories I had with him and forgave him for all he had done to me or the anguish he caused me. I found myself crying hours after his burial, repeating to everyone around me one comment I remember until now. 'If it were not for the Italian servants and associates, Queen Mother Nazly, and his mother-in-law Shwekar, Farouk would have been a different man and a different king.' I prayed for him, forgave him, and asked for God's forgiveness for him. My tears stopped, and I flew back to Beirut."

Farouk at his last dinner before his death, with his girl friend.

Farouk's funeral in Rome, among those present were his son Ahmed Fouad and his step sisters, Princess Feryal and Fwzyia.

As if in those few words, Farida was summarizing the whole history of that period, pointing the finger at those who, in her own eyes, were responsible for what happened to King Farouk and her life with him.

I asked Queen Farida, "What did you do when you heard of Farouk's death?"

She said, "When I heard that Farouk had just died, I flew immediately to Italy on March 17, 1965. As I learned, he died when he was having dinner at the Di France restaurant in Saint Trapeze hall in Rome. During that dinner, Farouk felt tired and exhausted, and all of a sudden, he passed out. Several attempts to resuscitate him by those at the restaurant failed, and he was immediately taken to the hospital. While Farouk was en route to the hospital, Dr. Nicola Massa put enormous efforts to revive him by massaging his heart to get it back to normal pulsation, but it was so weak, and the pulse became fainter and fainter until it stopped completely at one thirty that morning.

"Farouk was only forty-five years old when he died, and his body was kept at the morgue of the hospital, readying for burial in Egypt. On March 20, the body was transferred to one of the churches. It was wrapped with the old Egyptian flag. They held a simple funeral attended by his immediate family; his son, Prince Ahmed Fouad; our daughters, Princesses Feryal, Fawzyia, and Fadia; and his sisters, Fawzyia and Faiza. A few verses of the Quran were recited on his soul, as is traditional in Islamic funerals. After ten days, on March 27, the body was buried in Cairo, as I described earlier. After I returned to Beirut and as I looked at how the funeral procession was carried out with only few people in attendance in addition to his family, I began to ask myself, 'If he had just listened to me, would it have been different?' I guess we'll never know.

"The one thing that was troubling me in my mind was the way he died and where he passed. He did not die in his bed or his house. He died in the restaurant he loved most in Rome. I'll never know why it happened the way it did. And what is the lesson that comes out of it?"

Seeing all the sad emotions on Farida's face, I started to change the subject and asked her about her relationship with President Sadat.

"I met President Sadat at the Egyptian Embassy in Paris. He welcomed me so much that it drew everyone's attention. He also asked me to come back to live in Egypt. When I visited him at his house in Giza after going back to Egypt, he was very kind and complementary to me, as was his family as well. My story with President Sadat, however, was a different story!"

The Queen and President Sadat

"When I started to get settled in Paris and felt that life began to smile at me once more and my problems may now be over forever, my financial responsibilities started to haunt me again. The Shah of Iran had given me an apartment in Paris as a gift. This generous gift, however, had enormous costs attached to it, such as the property taxes and other maintenance expenses that I had to pay, along with my other daily expenses. Because of the size of the apartment, it needed a whole contingent of servants to care for it, adding more to my living expenses.

"With these mounting costs that I was responsible for, I decided to sell the apartment and rent a small studio instead. I was relieved from the exorbitant costs that I used to carry, and suddenly, my painting brushes began to move, my hand started to get stronger and stronger, and my art production began to increase. The studio I was living in was in a beautiful place in a great suburb, the one known as the sixteenth suburb in Paris, which I loved so much. I was happy with it, even though it was pretty small. I considered it as a gallery where I could paint my paintings. I kept only a few of my belongings, and at the end of the night, I had a place to sleep for a few hours. I was quite happy with that.

"The thought of establishing an art gallery in Paris, the world capital of the arts and the hub of all artists, was astounding to me. It was also the site of all that was new in the arts and the place where new schools for expressive art were born and new directions created. It was like a great dream for me. I thought I would begin to establish myself in the midst of all this beauty, and I decided to live right there in my gallery. While all of these thoughts were running in my mind and I was on the verge of making a lifelong decision, I received a dinner invitation from the Egyptian Embassy in Paris in honor of President Sadat, who was visiting Paris at the time.

"At the Egyptian Embassy and to my surprise, I was received with great attention and welcome. It was not the first time I received an invitation from the embassy, but this time, it was different from all my previous invitations. This time, I found myself face-to-face with President Sadat. He gave me a most hearty welcome and called his wife, the first lady. He introduced me loudly to her, saying, 'Queen Farida, Gehan. No one knows her history as much as I do. History will remember her for her great and patriotic roles that will never be forgotten.' Gehan welcomed me heartily as well, and President Sadat said, directing his comment to me, 'Isn't it time for you to come and settle in Egypt, the country you love and the one that loves you?' He squeezed hard on my hand. 'I'll be waiting for you in Egypt, and I'll see you next time in Cairo.'

"I was so happy for President Sadat and his wife's welcome. My happiness was so great because he invited me back to Egypt to settle there. My happiness could not be compared as I felt like a young girl who lived aimlessly all over the world and was now going back home. That was how I felt. I could not sleep and started thinking about President Sadat's offer. When the next morning came, that day felt and tasted differently, and I myself was like a new person, born again.

"I packed my bags and flew to Cairo, my beloved city with the eternal Nile that I adored. In Cairo, I was received with great fanfare from my oldest of friends. I felt as if I had been lost in the turmoil of life's struggles. Not too long thereafter, I had the son of one of my friends, Engineer Ahmed Hamdy, contact President Sadat's office to arrange for an appointment to meet with him and his family. I wanted to let him know that I was back in Cairo.

"Quickly, a meeting time was confirmed to meet President Sadat. It was set for noon, and I went early to the meeting, which was at the president's residence in Giza. The security of the residence welcomed me, and the president himself and his wife Gehan subsequently greeted me. I was so happy with that meeting, and the president kept praising me and my patriotic efforts during Farouk's time ever since we got married. He complimented me on being one of the principles that helped expose the corruption that was going on in the palace and how they controlled the king. Sadat was very gracious with me and gave me ample time for my visit with him and his family. I began to tell him about my love for the arts, the people I knew in Europe, and my life in general in Paris.

"The president interrupted and said, 'I hope you'll ask me for whatever you want or need. I'll make it happen immediately. You are Egypt's caring daughter, and on behalf of Egypt, I want to return some of your favors to the country. I want you to come back and settle down in your homeland, Egypt.'

"I thanked the president, Mrs. Sadat, and their family for their kind reception and interest in my well-being. I was happy many times more to return to my country with such welcome and care, especially that it was by the President of Egypt. It would reduce my earlier challenges that I contended with, roaming around different world capitals and working hard with my own hands to live my life and support myself.

"The president once again insisted and said, 'That is why I insist that you ask whatever you wish.' So I told him, 'I want to thank you for your invitation to come back and settle permanently in Egypt. It makes me so happy to do that. All I want is an apartment to live in because the government confiscated my palace by the Giza Pyramids, the one Farouk signed over to me after my divorce, even though I was outside the country and the laws did not apply.'

"President Sadat quickly answered, 'I want you to choose some other place, and I'll do it right away.' I thanked the president once more and said, 'I do not want the confiscated palace, and I do not want any other palace, not even a villa, as I cannot afford their expenses. All I want is an apartment overlooking the Nile, Egypt's great Nile, as Egypt and the Nile are the only two things that I love more than anything in my life.'

"President Sadat said, 'That is a modest request, and it is the least I can do for you, and I'll do it right away.' The president requested his office manager, Mr. Fawzy Abdel Hafez, to take care of this job and to have it furnished. He then turned to his wife Gehan. 'Gehan, you are responsible for making Queen Farida's request happen, following it up until the queen is settled in her apartment overlooking the Nile as quickly as possible.' He then turned toward me. 'You too consider Gehan as your sister in Egypt and ask of her whatever you want.'

"That day and after my visit with President Sadat and his family at Giza, I felt as if the world was still good in Egypt, represented by President Sadat, as I had two of my wishes answered: coming back to Egypt and having been given an apartment on the Nile.

"During that night, after leaving the president's house, I thanked God for his blessings onto me, and as I got out of the car, I kept looking at Egypt's eternal Nile, the glittering lights of the skyline shining on it and the waves changing the pattern of the glittering lights in a steady and beautiful rhythm. It was as if I were seeing the

Nile for the first time, as if I had not seen it before with this newfound beauty. So there I was, back to my great Nile.

"A few days later, the office of the president contacted me to see the apartment they had chosen for me. It was a beautiful place overlooking the Nile from all corners. I watched as though I was witnessing my dream come true with tears in my eyes. I thanked God for his great blessings onto me, and I told them that the apartment was just fine and beautiful. I then told them that they could proceed with the process to hand it over to me.

"When I later called Mrs. Gehan Sadat to thank her, she told me in a kind way that some obstacles had cropped up and there were some problems handing over the apartment to me. Such was my luck, as my dream of having an apartment on the great Nile never in fact materialized, even when I had the support of President Sadat, the president of Egypt."

"In God's Sanctuary," The Queen, a Guest of King Faisal

Seeking the Almighty

"When one's life and fate turn into a continuous journey of struggles and difficulties . . . when you cannot cope with anything around you . . . when you keep feeling that you have been dealt the wrong hand somehow, there is only one door left for you, and that is going back to God, going back to the only one who knows and understands where you have been and where you are going. It is God's open door of mercy for all his creation. It is there that God's care and his mercy touches you and becomes your closest ally in coping with all of life's difficulties."

At that moment, Queen Farida decided to travel to Saudi Arabia, do the Umrah, and seek God's help in directing her to the next phase in her life. The queen flew to Saudi Arabia as the guest of King Faisal and Queen Effat. Once there, she prepared for the Umrah and said, "My visit to Saudi Arabia brought back my emotional balance, and I was able to return to my faith in God. It was one of the best periods in my life. King Faisal was most hospitable with me to no end and asked about me a lot. I was very well received in the kingdom, and I was treated as a member of the royal Saudi family."

The king's generosity and care were tributes that left great impact on her and her life while performing the Umra, What Queen Farida remembered most were King Faisal's and Queen Effat's great attention and love for her and for hosting her at the Saudi great royal palace. She had a car for her personal services and all her local transportation as she needed.

"Throughout my stay in the kingdom, the royal Saudi family, especially Queen Effat, constantly took care of me. As it turned out, I actually had a family relationship with Queen Effat and formed a great and most affectionate friendship with her. I cannot describe what this Umrah did for me. I can say it changed my life and brought peace and serenity to my heart. I felt my warm tears coming down my face when I was circling the Kaaba, as if washing away all my sadness and sorrow that I had carried with me for so long. It brought me mental balance and deep faith in God.

Queen Farida harbored many memories of her visit to Saudi Arabia. One occasion was when she was invited to the royal wedding of Prince Abdallah, the king's son? She had to decline because she was not quite ready for such an event as she came only to perform the Umrah and had only simple daily clothing. Realizing that, Queen Effat quickly provided her with the appropriate attire so she could attend the royal wedding, which she did.

Queen Effat brought her private atelier and had her do whatever Queen Farida needed done to attend the wedding. With that, Queen Farida was able to attend all the private functions that the royal family was hosting. Frequently thereafter, Queen Effat asked about her well-being and kept in touch with her wherever she traveled, especially Paris, where Queen Farida decided to reside after leaving Egypt.

Farida's visit to the Saudi kingdom provided her with the hope that she was seeking by performing the Umrah. In fact, the king decided on a special pension for Queen Farida throughout her life. It was a great help to her overcoming some of her difficulties until she joined her daughters in Switzerland.

Queen Farida in Switzerland with her Daughters, Ferial, Fawzyia, and Fadia

Ironically, the princesses, Farida's daughters, resented their mother's actions and insistence on her divorce from their father, King Farouk. They insisted that her actions were responsible for the events that resulted in their father becoming a victim to his entourage of servants and profiteers. When she did not reconcile with their father, she was totally responsible for their living away so far apart and being unable to visit with her.

The fact of the matter, however, was totally different, as the corrupt palace lifestyle, the indecency of the king's court, and his assistants and servants were all under the control of Queen Mother Nazly. Queen Nazly made every effort to humiliate Farida for not having a son for the king. She paraded all the women who frequented the palace, all in spite of Farida. It did not matter if they were princesses or commoners. They were all under the influence of Princess Shwekar and her creation of the playboy environment that manifested itself around King Farouk. Not only that, it made life at the palace unbearable for Queen Farida. She began to feel the hatred and resentment of all those around her at the palace. The only thing Farida could do was turn inward onto herself. She was full of despair and could not do anything to rescue her husband, the king. It was like they were all falling into a sliding path for their own destruction and eventual loss of his throne.

She tried to be the good wife, caring and concerned about his reputation and that of the palace and the children. All her efforts, however, failed against the negative influences around the king, especially his mother, Queen Mother Nazly, and Princess Shewekar. There was no chance that she could continue her life with Farouk, and she insisted on her divorce at any cost. It became apparent to Queen Farida that the children were brainwashed, having lived with their father in exile, making her the evil one that was ultimately responsible for their divorce. The daughters were clearly in no condition to question their father's stories, which further widened the gap with their mother, especially that she was living far away from them.

When Queen Farida met with her daughters, she felt the awful distance between them. Their meeting did not have the warmth she had wished for and was looking forward to. There was that chill, just as the cold air you'd expect in Switzerland, that overcame their meeting and kept them apart, even during their brief encounter after so much time had lapsed since their father's exile. The bitterness Farida felt from her reunion with her daughters was visibly showing and became engrained in her memory ever since. She had set herself up for a warm and beautiful reunion, but her sorrow set in afterward. She could not rid herself of that for a long time.

She characterized her feelings about her meeting by saying, "My meeting with my three daughters left me with such a heavy burden that it was as if I was carrying the Great Pyramids on my head."

Farida's daughters had already built their own lives in Switzerland. Princess Fawziya owned a restaurant with her husband, where they both worked. Princess Feryal worked as a French schoolteacher in one of the Swiss schools, and Princess Fadia worked with her Russian husband in one of the horse breeding farms in Switzerland where he owned a few horses. The Egyptian princesses created that life for themselves outside Egypt. The heirs to the royal Egyptian monarchy were now married and earning their own keeps, working in a foreign land.

"Feryal had the major share of responsibility to take care of her sisters and her stepbrother, Ahmed Fouad. When Farouk was exiled, Feryal took in many responsibilities to take care of her father. Seeing the sadness and sorrow of her father, she had to take care of him and the rest of her family. After her father's divorce from his second wife Nariman, she also ended up taking care of her stepbrother, Ahmed Fouad, Nariman's son. Even at her young age, Feryal was like the mother to her sisters and brother. She declined many marriage proposals so she could take care of her younger brother until he became of age and was able to take care of himself.

"That was how they all ended up, having to take care of themselves and each other, working to make a living like everyone else, while in Egypt, you had the millionaires and billionaires thriving on the wealth of Egypt. It is a sad story in how it ended, but it all goes back to the common proverb that says, 'God gives it, and God takes it away.' It is all in God's wisdom, which you cannot challenge. It is a reminder to all those who think they have it all or know it all. They really do not."

"The Personal and the National Agony"

One day, we were having dinner at a London restaurant with heavy rains pouring outside under frigid temperatures. Queen Farida and I were talking about world issues, especially the Arab–Israeli war and the issue of Palestine.

Queen Farida said, "It was 1948, the year I can never forget, as it will always be etched in my memory until I die. It was May 15, 1948, when it was declared that the Egyptian armed forces would be taking part in the Arab–Israeli war. There was also my war in the capital. I was furious, as I witnessed the Egyptian youth, soldiers, and officers marching to war in Palestine to defend the rights of the Palestinians to their land in Palestine. The Zionist immigrants, fleeing the Nazi persecution in Germany, were taking Palestine. At that time, there was an unusual cooperation between the Egyptian political parties. While the palace was continuing their battles against me, the Egyptian army youth were fighting a war using guns that misfired, shooting back at them instead of the enemy.

King Farouk and Egyptian Army Chief of staff Haider
Basha, reviewing the progress in the Battle in Palestine.
King Farouk facial expressions, tell it all?

The corrupt palace service attendants and the fighting that
was going on hundreds of miles away in Palestine were constantly
challenging my feelings as a wife and a mother.

"My pains multiplied, and my mind was about to explode. I
was full of anguish as I heard about the crooked arms deals that
were taking place at the palace. The arms that were purchased were
later proven to have malfunctioned when the Egyptian soldiers and
officers used them. I heard a lot, even though I was supposed to be
kept out of the discussions, but I knew what was going on.

"The talk about the battles in the field and the losses that were mounting before the battles were even fought brought enormous despair in my heart and the hearts of all Egyptians. I felt as if my body was taking a beating much harder than the bullets in the battlefield. As my fate would have it, I was living two battles at the same time, the battle of my wounded nation and my personal battle at the palace.

"With the constant flow of news from the battlefront and the human losses that resulted, I could not sleep for nights at a time. Meanwhile, Farouk took residence with his court. He did not even have time to see his daughters. I was determined to do something. I had to be with the people and especially the wounded soldiers returning from the battlefield in Palestine. I started taking care of the soldiers and their families. I counseled them as well as the families of the martyrs who had no one to turn to. It was my way of sharing my sorrow with the grief of those families, and we became one. I helped and was also personally gratified through my small role counseling the returning soldiers and their families.

Queen Farida in route to a social benefit for the war victems.

"However, Farouk could not deal with it. He could not see me carving a role for myself, a role that gave me self-worth and comfort just by being with the people. He quickly decreed that I could not do that anymore. After being abandoned for so long, I decided not to be with him at any of the functions or events. Although people tried to get me to rescind my decision, I would not have it. I was certain that the king would not forgo being with his court and associates who were perpetrating their plans against the people. They convinced him that the majority of the Egyptians supported him and that the army was his protector. Little did he know that he was already being set up for his ultimate fall, and the Army Officer's Revolution soon followed."

Queen Farida was furious just for remembering as she reflected on that period and saw the events that took place throughout the war in Palestine. That was how she was, like a volcano, boiling on the inside when so many memories paraded before her eyes. The events rolled like a movie script in the back of her mind's eye. Then she would flare up so abruptly with immense anger for no apparent reason.

She then smiled and fondly remembered how the Egyptian people showed her how much they cared for and loved her. She could see and feel their support throughout her years with King Farouk during her marriage and after her divorce as well. "After the military revolution of 1952, the royal barrier evaporated, and the people's personal kinship to me became more overt, obvious, and outward. I could see and feel that wherever I walked in Cairo, even in the streets."

Farida said that with gleaning eyes, almost feeling the emotions of those days as if they were just happening.

Farida, The National Hero

The Egyptian people loved King Farouk. They loved him even more when he married Farida. But when she was divorced, people protested and went out in demonstrations, chanting in the streets against the corrupt palace and the immorality of what was happening inside it. The Egyptian people loudly chanted, "You left a house of irrepute and entered the house of nobility." That was how people chanted on the day of Farida's divorce from Farouk.

On November 17th, 1948, Farida's divorce became official. A royal decree announcing Farida's divorce from King Farouk was issued on that day. On the same day, as I mentioned before, another royal decree was issued announcing Queen Fawziya's divorce from the Shah of Iran. The announcements were arranged to take place at the same time to reduce the attention to Queen Farida's divorce. Irrespective of that, the Egyptian people demonstrated in the streets, marching against the king and supporting the queen. Farida suddenly became the people's hero, a national hero who was the victim of Farouk's corrupt court. Over the years, the people witnessed how she was the first to stand up against the crooked king's court. She was the first to expose the corruption and disgrace that was happening at the palace.

It became obvious to the Egyptian people that the king had surpassed all decency and used the People's Palace in the most obscene manner that could be imagined. Notwithstanding, the moral values of Islam, the respect for Al Azhar and the moral traditions of the whole country, Farouk's actions, and especially Farida's divorce constituted major triggers for massive demonstrations against the king and upholding Farida as the People's Queen.

Farida's divorce from Farouk was the first spark in the events that followed, which the military revolution of 1952 ended. It enflamed the emotions of the people and focused attention on the king's palace and what was happening inside it. The divorce suddenly broke the last barrier against the hidden corruption behind the palace walls. Farida was at the roots in every way that gave the national forces the opportunity to execute what eventually resulted in Farouk's exile from Egypt altogether on July 26, 1952.

"I had always given council to Farouk, but he disregarded it all. I gave him my counsel with full knowledge that the palace forces were working against me. Farouk would not listen, and he was eventually disgraced and exiled from Egypt. I could tell where everything was heading, but his insistence to follow his own path made me insist on getting my divorce. As a friend, I can tell you that asking for my own divorce was not easy for me, but it was a result of great suffering. My internal struggles were obvious to all around me. I did not want to seek my divorce. On the contrary, I was hoping to keep my personal link to my memories of the good times I had with Farouk in the initial years. At the same time, I wanted to stay away from Farouk and leave him to his corrupt staff and his doomed future. That was my quagmire and dilemma. I had feelings on both sides, wanting to cherish my good moments with Farouk and keep my family together while, at the same time, I could see that there was no hope in rescuing my marriage. It had just gone so far for any possible repair. Divorce was the only way I could keep my respect and avoid the torture that had befallen me from all that I lived through.

"When I asked for my divorce, Farouk was in a state of shock and disbelief. He could not imagine that I was serious about it. Farouk was also going through hard times and thought that my request for divorce was only a threat, nothing more. Farouk actually cried when he signed the divorce decree. He sent so many intermediaries to get me to agree to stay on and forget the divorce, but to no avail. My determination was solid, and I insisted on staying out of his way altogether. I did not want to be seen anywhere he was so he would be forced to sign my divorce papers.

"When all the divorce documents were signed and my divorce became official, Farouk disappeared. He simply went out of sight, and no one could tell where he was until his daughters found him in a room by himself, weeping like a child."

He truly loved Farida, and the divorce did not settle in until he actually signed the official papers. Farouk was depressed for a long time after the divorce. His only counsel was his staff, especially his Italian servants who celebrated the occasion. Now they had succeeded in getting their long-held wish, getting rid of Farida who did everything in her power to discredit them and to save her husband from their disgraceful networks. They had nothing better to offer than search for prostitutes for him from all the nightclubs around.

Among his strange habits was that he had a secret room built by the swimming pool in the palace, specifically situated to watch the ladies in their swimsuits from below. This was all done without the knowledge of the ladies in the pool. That was how life in the royal palace used to be, anything and everything for the pleasure of the king.

Since Farida's divorce from Farouk, she became a role model for her daughters, in fact for all Egyptian wives. She became the model of the woman who would give up her secure life and fortune rather than live with a cheating husband. Not only did Queen Farida give up her secure royal lifestyle, she also gave up her crown. As the former queen of Egypt, she relinquished all the power and prestige that went with being the queen and first lady of Egypt. She refused to be the queen for a king who had no respect for the honor of his wife, the queen; for his family and daughters; and especially for his citizens, the Egyptian people.

Farida knew she was making a decision that would significantly impact her life and make it most difficult, a life that could not be tolerated except for the most hardy and strong of people. She remembered the poet who wrote, "When the Souls were strong and grand . . . there; the Bodies suffered in return."

Queen Farida could have chosen to work from behind the scenes, rule the palace court, and instigate what she could, and no one would have known. She had the power to destroy Farouk and expose him to the people and get rid of the entire king's court, but that was not like her. That was not Farida. She was a different person who could not be compared on the same level as those who fought her.

"Unfortunately, Farouk was a spoiled king. He had the least amount of education, especially as he was rushed back home from

England after his father's death to be crowned as king of Egypt. When King Fouad passed away, Farouk was only sixteen years old. During his early life, few women, namely his mother, Queen Mother Nazly, and his sisters, greatly influenced Farouk. Farouk did not have a chance to interact with his peers, a matter that kept him from maturing to become a king and a ruler of a country like Egypt.

"These factors combined had a lot to do with the way Farouk ended up, a young, impressionable adolescent whose elders could manipulate. It is no wonder that, as he grew older, he became a playboy king who had no concept of marital duties or responsibilities. He was fully under the guidance of his mother, who had only one concern in her life, getting an heir to the throne, Farouk.

"No wonder that when the 1952 revolution took place, it happened quickly with no confrontation whatsoever, and his exile was uneventful. He was gone for good, and he only came back to Egypt in the middle of the night as a corpse to be buried in Egypt thirteen years after his exile."

"Ahmed Fouad, the Son I Did Not Have"

"Ahmed Fouad, the son I did not have." With these words, Queen Farida continued her story. She described her daughters' lives in Switzerland with sadness, how they received her and how they told her that all the difficulties and pain in their lives were caused by her.

"Kids are not the same anymore. These days, they do things in a much different way than in the old days. They are a different generation not like ours. We knew how to conduct ourselves in the proper way." There was a long moment of silence. "Although God did not give me a son, which was the main reason for my problems with Farouk and led to my divorce, I felt that Ahmed Fouad was like the son I did not have. After my divorce, Farouk married Nariman, who gave him his son, Ahmed Fouad. On the morning of July 26, 1952, Ali Maher, then the prime minister of Egypt, received a military demand note from General Mohamed Nageib that King Farouk was to relinquish the throne to his son Ahmed Fouad by noon that day and that, if he did not comply, he, Farouk, would have to bear the consequences.

"It was almost like the confrontation of February 1942 when the British ambassador, Sir Miles Lampson, threatened Farouk and surrounded the Abdeen Palace with the British troops and tanks. At that time, Farouk only had to change the Egyptian cabinet and give the prime minister's position to the Wafd party. Farouk complied and the impasse was averted. This time, however, it was a different situation. His military officers, the Council of Egyptian Revolutionary Officers, were handing in the note to abdicate.

"It was before day's end, around five thirty that afternoon, close to sunset, that the crew of *Al-Mahrousa* saw Queen Nariman with her son Ahmed Fouad and the three princesses, Feryal, Fawzyia, and Fadya, sailing toward the yacht. Ahmed Fouad had just become the king of Egypt at noon that day. He was only two years old when he became the uncrowned king of Egypt. His father had just relinquished the throne to him by order of the Military Revolutionary Council. Ahmed Fouad was the king of Egypt in absentia for less than a year, 1952 through 1953. Egypt was declared a republic on June 18, 1953, and the monarchy was forever gone.

"Now, Ahmed Fouad is forty years old and lives in Paris with his Turkish wife. They were married, and their wedding was held at the royal palace in Monaco. The prince of Monaco was a good friend of Farouk. It was a great wedding with all the celebrities, royalties, princes, and princesses in attendance. All came from the far corners of the globe to take part in that special wedding. The royal couple afterward settled in Paris.

Prince Ahmed Fouad with his mother, Former
Queen Nariman, during a visit in Egypt.

"I remember well when his wife Fadya became pregnant and was about to have a baby. That day, Ahmed Fouad requested from President Sadat to allow his wife to have their baby in Egypt. They called him Mohamed Ali after their great-great grandfather, Mohamed Ali the Great, whose dynasty ruled Egypt from 1805 through 1952.

"A similar request was done for their second child as well. Ahmed Fouad was keen to stay in touch with what was happening in Egypt, never really separating himself from the events that were happening in Egypt while he was living in Paris. He was primarily involved in what was going on with the Mohamed Ali family in Egypt, especially his father's holdings. Ahmed Fouad actually appeared in a French movie, which was made for television, produced, and directed by a good friend of his, Fredrick Mitterrand, the nephew of François Mitterrand, the French president. The film was about Farouk and the period when he was the king of Egypt. The French television actually showed the movie twice, once in the morning and another time at prime time in the evening. Ahmed Fouad appeared in the film and made comments on the movie events afterward.

Ahmed Fouad's name was also noted several times in the Arab and foreign press. It was rumored that he was behind El-Ryan investments. The implication was that he was the investor who bought the real estate and various companies that were part of El-Rayan holdings. El-Rayan Holding's Company came to the limelight after thousands of average Egyptians poured their life savings into the company for promised high returns, which the company later was not able to keep. The company went into bankruptcy, and the investment turned out to be a major scam, bringing enormous losses to thousands of average unsuspecting Egyptians. Ahmed Fouad was working behind the scene, represented by the buyer's attorney, Rashad Nabieh Esquire.

In June 1991, Ahmed Fouad's name was prominently featured in the Egyptian press. This time, it was for his attendance in the wedding of his stepbrother, Tarek El-Naquib, and to check on his mother's health. Nariman, Ahmed Fouad's mother, was living at the time in Heliopolis, a suburb of Cairo. On this visit, Ahmed Fouad also visited the new opera house and some of the national antiquities in Cairo. Minister of Culture Farouk Housny gave him a limited tribute dinner in his honor. That dinner raised some eyebrows and chatter in the society circles, as if there were more to it than actually was.

Queen Farida considered Ahmed Fouad as her son, even though his mother was Nariman, Farouk's second wife. She always visited with him in Paris, where he accompanied her throughout her visits. He took care of her while in Paris, taking her to lunches and dinners.

They had a close relationship with each other. He used to ask her about what many in the news media were saying about his father, talking about his failings and even addressing the way he ate. It annoyed him greatly when he was a child when his schoolmates teased him about the media references to his father "eating like a pig." He would be very annoyed with these references and did not know what to do, other than sharing them with Farida in search for answers.

Farida had no answer, and she was actually as much annoyed with these references as Ahmed was. He was like a real son for her, and his pains affected her greatly. It was a relationship that had a lot of caring and respect on both sides.

Queen Farida once said, "I feel bad for Nariman. She was a victim as I was. She is not a bad person, and I pray for her recovery. She has the same disease as I do. May God give her the best of health and a swift recovery."

Queen Farida's first meeting with Queen Nariman was very tense and filled with high emotions. Queen Farida had ended her self-exile in Europe and came back to Egypt, filled with thousands of memories, happy ones as well as sad. Farida had decided to hold her first art show in her homeland, Egypt. She specifically chose the Meridian Hotel for her exhibit. The Meridian Hotel is built as a round structure directly on the Nile. Hotel visitors cannot miss the grand panoramic view of the Nile from any corner or room at the site.

The show was a success, and a great many art enthusiasts from all over Egypt attended. There were the dignitaries and government ministers, as well as regular Egyptians and art critics. All came to appreciate her work as well as her struggle. These people loved her and prayed for her when she was going through hard times with Farouk. The show was like a referendum from the people. Everyone came to show their love and appreciation of the people's queen artwork. It was a historical moment for Farida that she could not forget.

While attending to all the festivities, meeting people, showing and talking about her artwork, everyone congratulating her, and celebrating her return to her homeland, suddenly she was face-to-face with Queen Nariman. This was the first meeting they had, a meeting between the two queens of Egypt, Farida and Nariman. While surprised by Queen Nariman's unexpected appearance at her art show, Queen Farida hugged her and asked about her health and her personal life, all with great anticipation and fondness. As they toured the show together, Farida described her artwork to Nariman, who listened intently.

Farida said, "When I saw Nariman, the memories quickly came back, bringing the difficult years that passed when we both had difficult times. I remembered a lot that reflected the hard times and sad memories, but I harbored no ill feeling toward Nariman. I wished her the best, as she was like me, a helpless victim for the events that were much more powerful than we could deal with.

"Now, Nariman lives in a modest apartment in Heliopolis, suffering from her illness. May God relieve her pain and hasten her recovery. Nariman had a great time when she came with her son to visit me. Ahmed Fouad was in town at the time of the wedding of Tarek El Naquib, his stepbrother."

Farida's heart could not bear grudges against anyone. Her soft and kind heart was always forgiving. She could not have any ill feelings about Farouk, even after they were divorced. She would not hear it when people talked badly about Farouk's behavior or his chasing of women. She always reminded those people, saying, "Farouk is dead, and you are now talking about the history of a deceased man, so leave him alone. Each of us has his good deeds and bad ones, so let him rest in peace."

In fact, Ferial, Farida's oldest daughter, actually took care of Ahmed Fouad during his early years while growing up. While Ahmed Fouad was her stepbrother, Ferial sacrificed a lot for him, declining many engagement offers and other marriage possibilities. She felt it was her duty to take care of him, just as his mother would have. Queen Nariman, at the time, was living in Egypt and had married Dr. El-Naquib.

The turns of the Egyptian history are like a continuous chain of events, sometimes plagued with horrors and misfortunes and, at times, filled with brilliant historical achievements. All together, they form unyielding pages of history that remain there with the truths. When history is written, there is no mercy, kindness, or bias. All but the bare facts remain for the following generations to study and to contemplate.

Farida's divorce from Farouk and the exposé that followed constituted significant elements in what would take place later. Whether intentional or unintentional, Queen Farida had an inner capability to analyze the events of her time. When she observed the rampant corruption in the palace and the rude behavior of her husband the king, she could only see that the end was near.

She could see that the corruption that was going on in the palace, day in and day out, was not sustainable. Especially after the botched arms deals of 1948, she saw that the system would surely fall. It did and precisely for the reasons she saw. If justice were the basis of good governance, evil and corruption would only bring failure and disgrace. After all, it was all in God's hands. He gives it and takes it away. God's mercy will only be given to those who deserve it, and God's punishment will be for those who choose the wrong path, the path of corruption and poor judgment.

The Queen and Egyptian Heritage

Queen Farida had a distinct appreciation for ancient art and culture. She also had a fascination with modern architecture, especially that of the world-renowned Egyptian architect Hassan Fathy.

Farida said, "Hassan Fathy is a national treasure in the arts and philosophy of architecture. To have an Egyptian architect with his understanding and knowledge is an awesome feat for Egypt and the Arab world. The manner in which he blends his architectural works with the environment is exemplary. I must say that he is no less than the dean of architecture in Egypt and the Arab World.

"I was once invited to a dinner event at Hassan Fathy's house in Darb El Labbana near the old castle. At the dinner were many dignitaries, like the American and Turkish ambassadors and many Arab diplomats. The rarest of designs that showed the Egyptian and Arabic heritage filled the house. You could see the Arabesque pieces with their inlays of rare shell designs, the wooden furniture that fit so well in the house décor. The old Turkish designs and famed Arabic Mashrabiya stood out, giving the house an immense Arabian feel.

"Hassan Fathy, the architect and host, was waiting upstairs on the second floor, which he dedicated for the bedrooms. The first floor was a reception for his guests. Two hours before the guests were to arrive and while Hassan Fathy was still in the upstairs quarters, the stairs connecting the first and second floors suddenly collapsed. There was no time for him to repair the stairs in time for the guests' arrival. He ended up having to greet his guests from the second floor. It was difficult to correct the situation in time or for him to be brought down, being at an age he could not risk making any such moves, so he greeted his guests and gave his talk from the second floor while his guests watched and listened from below.

"Even with that, the evening was full of laughter and pleasant conversations. Everyone had a great time, teasing him at times that he should not stay upstairs while his guests were on the first floor. Out of respect for him, however, everyone stayed on and entertained themselves to a great traditional meal made up of fool medames (fava beans), falafel, pickles, and the like. It was a great fun evening, even with the host not able to give his personal presence, except from the second floor."

The international reputation of Hassan Fathy was the pride of the Egyptian people. Queen Farida was proud that such an Egyptian architect was of that caliber and at the top of his profession. He was indeed an Egyptian national treasure. Many world leaders, including William R. Bollk, the head of the Adlai Stevenson Institute for Foreign Affairs, had great appreciation of Hassan Fathy's works. Farida was a true artist with great understanding of the different fields of art. Hassan Fathy was one example that brought a new field of Egyptian architecture to the world, and the world had only praise for his talent and designs.

In an article about Hassan Fathy in February 2012, "Hassan Fathy is the Middle East's Father of Sustainable Architecture," Green Prophet sums up his works noting, "Hassan Fathy, an Egyptian architect, saw the value of natural building long before it became a fad in the west."[2]

---

2   http://www.greenprophet.com/2010/02/hassn-fathy-sustainable-architecture

Land, "The Pride and Honor of Every Egyptian Farmer"

"When I was asked during one of my art shows in 1985 why I did not have paintings of the farmlands around Egypt, I did not know what to say. The fact of the matter was that I had a great affection for our beautiful countryside. Since my early days with Farouk, when he and I eloped to Anshas, my love for the village and village life, the farms, and the beautiful green landscape really began. That was when I had my best two weeks with Farouk, right after our wedding. I always saw the countryside filled with hospitality, generosity, and purity. But that countryside had changed over the years. I could no longer see the beautiful green landscape, but I saw buildings instead. I did not find the simple farmer who used to get up at dawn to farm his land. Instead, I saw the farmer who was running after money in any way he could, away from working his farm, the way his fathers and grandfathers cared for it for thousands of years.

"I did not see the simple farmer's wife who used to get up with her husband to bake the bread and go to the field to help him farm the land. Instead, I found the wife who, instead of raising her chicken and other small animals to help her husband, waited for the bread to come from the automated bakeries, and the meat and produce came from the supermarket. I saw the farmer's family watching colored television and encouraging her husband to leave farming for a life in the city. It was sad for me to see the loss of the pride and honor that farmers used to have for their farmland exchanged for the city life that he could not afford.

"These drastic changes were quite a shock to me and caused me great anxiety and deep sorrow for how life has changed in the Egyptian countryside. This feeling had a great impact on my art and was the reason I did not have as many paintings of the villages and the countryside as I would have liked to.

"I showed the farmer in my paintings as a surreal image from the past. That was what I had in my memory. I hesitated many a time between the old and the new. I did not despair, however, and always had hopes that things would come back to what the old countryside used to be. I continued to hope that the countryside would come back to its beauty and give the farmer the pride and honor he used to have. I am comforted now that the government has started to make changes to prevent the destruction of the farmland and introduced laws to prevent the willful conversion of farmland to real estate developments. Because of these changes, I showed in one of my paintings the hesitant farmer who came back to his land after being through the vicious cycle of the city life. I called that piece, 'Return to Earth.'"

Egypt, the Cradle of the Arts

"I focused my attention to my art and my love to my country. I loved the simple Egyptians who gave me their passion and covered me with their kindness. I loved how they expressed their feelings to me, how they covered me with their warmth and surrounded me with their love. I remember my uncle, Judge Mahmoud Said, who taught me to focus my attention to art and painting. He told me, 'Put whatever comes to your mind on your canvas. It is the best expression of your state of mind.' It was so true. Painting was always my best reprieve, where my inner self came out in my art. It gave me the chance to forget, even for a time, my difficulties at the palace."

Judge Mahmoud Said was one of the leading figures that established modern art in Egypt. His family was one of the most respected and rich families in Alexandria. He lived near Morsi Abou-El-Abbas Mosque. Born in Alexandria on April 8, 1897, he received a French law degree in 1919, the year of the first Egyptian revolution. Mahmoud Said also studied art at the most distinguished art schools in Paris, including the famous art institute, the Julian Academy. After his return, he joined the prosecutor's office in the International Court in Mansoura while continuing his passion with art. Subsequently, Judge Mahmoud Said focused on his legal profession, excelling in it and advancing to become a justice of the International Court in Cairo.

The Egyptian way of life and personality clearly influenced Judge Said's artwork. He examined Egyptian art going back to its earliest times in Egyptian history. The influence of the Islamic and Pharaonic art were clear in his artistic expressions. One of Said's great works was his painting of the launching of the Suez Canal at the time of Khedive Ismail. He also had a lot of works in which he concentrated on painting family and friends, including one painting of Queen Farida in her early years.

Mahmoud Said's artworks reached the highest of international acclaim. Auctions of many of his paintings and artworks at Christie's, the famed international auction house, were a testament of his enormous success and stature as an Egyptian artist and accomplished painter. Auctions of his paintings sold for hundreds of thousand Egyptian pounds and dollars. His acclaim continued after his death in 1964. In recognition of his art, an Egyptian art museum was established in his honor, where many of his works are on exhibit, in Cairo.[3]

Queen Farida continued, "He was an excellent expressionist, fascinated with paintings of the common Egyptian woman in her folkloric dress. He was awarded the Egyptian National Achievement Award. After his death in 1964, the Egyptian government dedicated a museum in his name to honor him and include his works. This is the Mahmoud Said Art Museum in Al-Gezira district of Cairo.

"Even with all my love and fondness for my uncle Mahmoud Said's art, I made every effort not to follow his school in the arts. I wanted my own expressions; I wanted to develop my own school unaffected by others. Having said that, his focus on the Egyptian way of life and documenting it in his artworks still influenced me. With that, I continued with my painting style, which took its roots from my own state of mind. I maintained my personal differences and my own expressions in my artwork."

---

[3]   www.christies.com/lotfinder/paintings/mahmoud-said-sunset-on-the-nile-at-5305193-details.aspx; https://www.google.com/search?q=mahmoud+saeed+artist&tbm=isch&tbo=u&source=univ&sa=X&ei=NCktUpu6Do-44APwhoDYCw&sqi=2&ved=0CC8QsAQ&biw=960&bih=482

"Paris, the Birthplace of My Life in the Arts"

"France, especially Paris, was where my life in the arts actually began. It was where I had my first art exhibit of my work. It brought me happiness and a feeling of belonging to the art community in Paris. At the beginning, I did not have a place I could call my own. However, as soon as I began to settle down, the news of my presence in Paris came to the attention of the Shah of Iran, who was kind enough to buy me an apartment for my own use, as a gift to me.

"Once I had my own place and created my own studio to do my artwork, I began to feel the comfort of settling down. All of a sudden, friends and acquaintances in the arts enriched my life. My artwork had its own following, and life began to smile at me. It brought me enormous pleasures to just organize my canvas, my paint, and paintbrushes, along with other art tools, in my own studio. It helped me learn the intricacies of the different art techniques in none other than the capital of the arts in the world, Paris.

"Almost on a daily basis, I frequented the art stores and districts in Paris and purchased what I needed to develop my art techniques. I began to dedicate a lot of my time to art. I began to develop the confidence I needed to visit the many art schools, learn the different types of art techniques, and understand the colors and where they had the best meaning and impact. It was a new life for me, full of learning and discovery. I had everything I needed to develop my talent in the arts, surrounded by the experts who did not know me but were willing to help me and teach me the essence of the different techniques of the arts.

"As time went by and the cost of living in Paris began to rise, I started to spend more and more of my income, not only for my living expenses, but also on my art supplies and needs. As you know, art is an expensive hobby, especially when you want to do it at a professional level. There were also lots of taxes, and as if that were not enough, the French government started to introduce property tax assessments on real estate. My apartment, although the Shah had gifted it to me, was taxed heavily to a point where I could not keep up with it. I had no alternative but to sell it and devote all my time to my art.

"I worked very hard to produce enough of my paintings to open my first art exhibit in Paris. I was so scared and full of anxiety, worried about the success or failure of the exhibit. I wanted so much for it to be well received. After all, it was my first attempt in Paris to show my friends and my art colleagues my work. In 1970, I studied the history of French art at the Louvre. I studied lithography at the Mourlouth, better known as Toulouse-Lautrec. I even took classes at the Regal Atelier to learn about metal sculpture.

"I started to use novel and uncommon tools, making use of lighting in ways that were different from the norm. I was not quite sure if these variations would be accepted, especially that I was in the midst of the art center of the world. Deep inside, however, I wanted to succeed in Paris. I felt that, if my art was accepted in Paris, it would be the best testament to the quality of my art. It would, in fact, be a declaration of the birth of my art career. I was under enormous pressure, and I put every ounce of my energy into it to succeed.

"When the opening day of my art exhibit came, I could not imagine that it would be received the way it was received. A large number of my friends and art colleagues came to the exhibit. People whom I studied with or was mentored by, owners of the schools I studied at, were all there. The reception my work got from all who came through amazed me. The comments I received about my art and the special appeal it had were so warm. It made me feel like I was on cloud nine.

"The exhibit succeeded beyond my imagination. The reception I had from everyone was almost like a wedding reception with all the festivities and joy that comes with it. I truly felt like a professional artist, and my artwork became a source of income for me. With that, my artwork helped support my living expenses in Paris. I lived my best and happiest days in Paris, surrounded by friends and artists alike. It was the kind of a dream life that one does not plan for. It just happens. I felt that life was smiling at me once again, and I was not about to let it go this time. I wanted to savor the moments, every single one of them.

Queen Farida hard at work with her canvas,
readying for her Art Show in Paris'

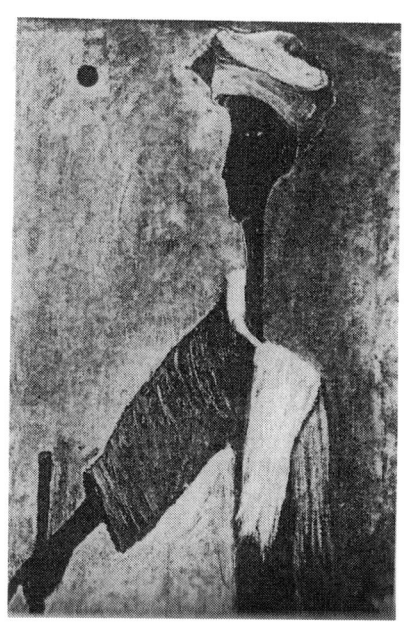

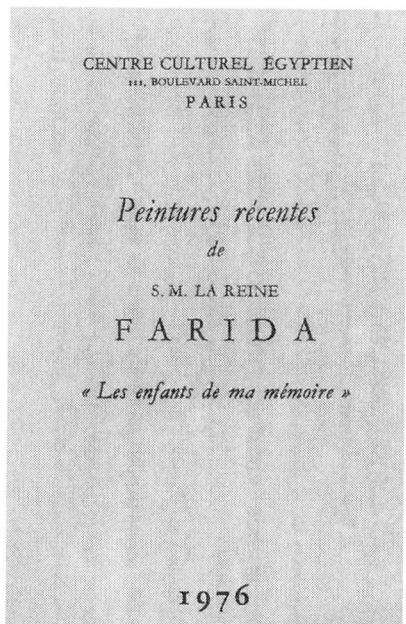

CENTRE CULTUREL ÉGYPTIEN
111, BOULEVARD SAINT-MICHEL
PARIS

Peintures récentes
de

S. M. LA REINE

F A R I D A

« *Les enfants de ma mémoire* »

1976

Queen Farida's Invitation Card for her Art Exhibit in Paris, 1976.

Samples of Queen Farida's art production clearly attesting
to talent and attachment to her country, Egypt.

Reviews of Farida's Art

Claude Rachel

"The new artwork by Queen Farida shows a unique presentation form that crystallizes the scene and connects with the viewer in a manner that attracts viewers to the exhibit. After the first shock of witnessing the new style of the artist and the different expressions brought into the artwork, through new advances and technological innovations, it is as if the subjects in the picture are actually moving in front of one's eyes. The scene of the Egyptian countryside with its houses and livestock, the sun in the backdrop, and the ectoblastic figures in view are dealt with with great skill. It projects the artist's capability of transmitting her continued anxiety through the images she projects in her expressive art. This takes away the unknown and provides more of the simplicity and strength in her work. Like many other established artists, she shows her exceptionalism through her new portraits that will withstand the test of time. The artwork presented in 1984 carries new vistas demonstrating the centrism in her new art. It is truly a great feat that she is back to her art gallery with the glittering colors and the magical representation of the farm girls walking with beauty on the banks of the Nile.

"While our eyes flirt with the grand beauty of the artwork, it attests to the keen fondness of the artist to her homeland through the light reflections against the beautifully colored Nile waters in a special poetic theme. It is from this that one gets a multitude of impressions representing the many elements and forms in her art. With a more critical examination of the artwork, you'll see the blending of the many facets, social and artistic, in a mosaic that touches the inner senses of the viewer. It almost numbs the sense of the portraits through the alternation of the spotlights on the portrait in an ensemble that touches the inner feelings of the viewer. We are transferred to an unknown world combined with the subconscious taking it out of the doldrums.

"The artist's use of Cenitism, where she studied the use of spotlights with their alternating moves that in turn create continuity of perception with the human eye, completing her search and replacing the architectural form through the deep valleys of the subconscious, is all interconnected in the subconscious of the moment."

Jan Marchamian

"Farida came to give this stone deaf world a few shades of her transparent dream, a voice that gives it life. She shows the desire to transform the real into the magical. You cannot compare her portraits to any other."

Patrick Waldberg

"Farida stays away from the superficial to bring us close to her inner beauty. The artwork that we see shows her inspiration and extensive desires through her vibrant thoughts and Oriental spirit."

Jan Mackwelly Claud

"The voice of the artist carries with it her message through her clever use of objects and colors. The deep vision in some portraits and other works is the mystery she portrays. There is something that is transparent and indirect as though hanging over, yet it is solid and stable at the same time."

Fred Broute

"The human spirit, the visible objects, and the living forms in her portraits are the primary sources of expression that radiate throughout her work. That is what distinguishes Farida's work from all others. It is you, the bright star that came from Egypt. You are the one who maintained all the brilliance of RAA3's light on the sands of Egypt. Everything is lit like the laser beam, showing people and artifacts conjoined with their souls. Like combining together the hidden and unseen yet omnipresent and beating with life. It is like an angel that fell, looking over its fallen, lifeless body, full of reality and truths, at the height of transparency and brilliance of colors. Your portraits demand one's deep thoughts and contemplation."

Excerpts from the International Press Reviews

The international press also covered Farida's exhibit. Some of these press reviews and comments are shown below:

For the first time in Paris, an astonishing experiment in the expressive art was introduced, an experiment that can be described as revolutionary. If we take into account that contemporary art has achieved unusual highs, what Farida has reached has created a new level of expressive art, which she introduced through variations in her lighting techniques.

Mary Pyros

"Farida conceptualized her new artwork from the constant presence of the peasants. She invented a better and more distinct way of interpreting the human face. Using this interpretation, she was able to envisage the deep meaning of Egypt and, with that, glorifies her country in an honorable way."

Maneek Presel Droway

"The queen's portraits inspire greatness, mystery, and brilliance. On a sunny and beautiful day, many of Queen Farida's art lovers attended an exhibit at the Continental Hotel where she was surrounded by her friends and admirers. She captured the attention and admiration of all around her with her esteemed presence, her intellectual capacity and knowledge, her beautiful smile, and kindness. But of course, with these thousands of her art admirers, getting close to her art pieces was next to impossible. However, viewing her portraits the following days in the quiet atmosphere of the art exhibit allowed for a close inspection of her methods of expression in her art. They were distinctive with their lighting patterns and the colors that were assembled together with elegance and precision. Through these modern expressive techniques, her art captured a great deal of free and distinctive expression. Queen Farida concentrates on using her lines in and out of the portrait as is necessary to reach the brilliant limits of her colors. The magical life in the Far East in some of the queen's portraits gives the impression of greatness and mystery at the same time. However, the portraits show her personality in a clear way. Queen Farida, who continued to paint since 1954 without tiring, became a professional artist through her closeness to her artwork."

James Rafealle Soto and Francois Moucilay

"My research through the last ten years led me to Cenitism, the clear or apparent light movement that the eye sees. The main problem that confronted the expressionist artists was identifying each hour of the day or night, reflecting its sequenciality. I worked hard to assemble all the periods in the portrait from sunrise to sunset and back. I limited the use of light sources to two lamps, one was vertical, representing the sun at noon at ninety degrees. And the other was on the side, representing sunrise or sunset at 180 degrees. In a completely dark room, we observed the light changes using a variable electronic apparatus or Dynamo. These changes produced a number of warm and cold lights, which in turn showed the image variations without the colors and showed its vibrant movements in a perfect musical ensemble. For me, each movement was spontaneously generated through our interaction with the universe and consolidation with it. These constant oscillations, which are produced in harmony, brought us in an association with light as the eternal source."

Farida and Her Life in the Arts

Queen Farida grew up in an artistic environment, surrounded by her artist relatives. When she was young, she used to watch her uncle, the renowned artist Mahmoud Said, whom she used to watch by attentively observing his moves as he painted. That was when she developed a sense and a liking for the arts. She also had an innate talent for the arts and would watch her uncle's brush strokes and follow every movement he made on his canvas. She learned the different schools of art and the different types of artistic expressions. Farida kept away her inner feelings toward her uncle's art productions, wanting to have an opportunity to develop her own style when she grew up. Farida wanted to express her emotions and her feelings toward life and the people around her on her own canvas and through her own brush strokes and colors.

Her growing up in Alexandria, the second capital of Egypt and the most beautiful city on the southern shores of the Mediterranean Sea, also influenced Farida's love for the arts. Before her marriage to King Farouk, she spent her teens in Alexandria watching the clear blue waters of the sea and the majestic radiant colors as they developed at sunset. It was the majestic view that develops every day at sunset when the huge, round disk of the red sun slowly sinks at the horizon into the waters of the Mediterranean. If you combine that with the cloud variation in the sky, the images are just incredible. Each image for each day can actually produce amazing natural portraits that could not be duplicated on any artist's canvas.

All of these emotions and images became engraved in Farida's memory that reflected in her paintings. Using her unique colors and the light reflections on her artwork, she was able to formulate the most beautiful and romantic appeal in her portraits. Her lighting arrangements, as projected on her artwork, brought out incredible feelings for anyone viewing her artwork. Her paintings gave different perspectives under the morning sun from those at sunset. She complemented these images at night using soft direct and indirect spotlights on her paintings.

With that, Farida developed her own exhibition style and art presentation. What characterized her artwork further was the additional hint of lighting perfection that made her artwork stand out and her paintings look like being adorned by a characteristic lighting scheme that was only Farida's.

Her paintings of the sailboats floating on the Nile with the sunset behind them from afar, the flapping sails and the dancing boatmen, are all in a presentation that creates so much realism and vitality in the painting. They brought real life and dancing right to the canvas for the viewer to enjoy. The red sun, though far in the background, provides the center of gravity for the whole painting and adds delicate beauty to Farida's artistic expressions.

Many times, I watched Queen Farida viewing her own art at the exhibitions. I saw her standing for a long time in front of each painting. It was as if she was undressing the painting with her own piercing eyes, watching the beauty that is in front of her. I could also see through her facial expressions how each painting brought back memories so vividly, as if she was reliving those moments once again. There was no doubt that these paintings by themselves were the documentaries to her life with its happy and sad moments expressed in her artwork.

Farida excelled in her art, especially when she lived in Paris and interacted with the art crowd that flocked to the art capital of the world to learn from each other. It was there that she studied the many schools of art expression. That was also where she felt that her art became her life. It became the medium through which she could forget her difficult times with Farouk while rejoicing her sweet moments with him at the same time.

At her art exhibit in Bahrain, she told me, "I want people to know what I want to say."

Looking at the clown painting with all its brilliant colors in the costume of the dancing figure under the varying lights was her way of screaming out to the world with her inner emotions expressed beautifully in the colorful dress of the clown and the tears running down his sad face. She called the painting "Life." That was what life was like for her, a mixture of love and joy, mixed in with the many struggles she went through fighting for her rights and the rights of her daughters in the corrupt palace.

One could see the contrasting expressions in her paintings without exception, reflecting her life's experiences, bare of all pretense and falsehood. That was her way of excelling in her art presentations. She knew that, when an artist expresses himself or herself in a true and authentic fashion, the outcome could only be a great one. That was how Farida produced her art.

"I start my paintings with a few brush strokes of different colors and shades. Soon thereafter, the painting takes its own life, and I would be just filling in from my soul. The rest of the painting suddenly comes out to life, as if I was in a dream."

Queen Farida at the opening of her Art Exhibit in
Bahrain, with Bahrain's Prince and Farouk Hashem.

At the exhibit, Queen Farida came to one particular painting and
stopped. "This painting is very dear to my heart. I would not sell it
for any price. This painting represents the Arab world with all of its
potential and resources. If these resources were put to proper use,
they could create a brilliant future for its people."

She called that painting "The Arab Giant." It was her vision
of what the Arab world could do if its people rose from their safe

havens and worked to achieve their hidden potential. If they did, it would be for the betterment of its people from the East to the West and from the North to the South, providing freedom, opportunity, and justice to all.

The Queen and the Prince

On October 19, 1986, the Bahraini government invited Queen Farida and me to do an art exhibit for Farida's artworks. When we arrived at the Manama Airport, we were received at the VIP lounge, and we sat together while waiting for the clearance of the queen's art pieces from the plane. In a few minutes, we were on our way in a large motorcade to the Diplomat Hotel. A separate caravan of cars was taking the artwork to the royal palace. Another fleet of cars was taking the television personnel and reporters to their hotels.

While we sat down in the queen's special suite at the Diplomat Hotel, she told me, "This is my first motorcade since my divorce from Farouk. This is a royal motorcade I have not had for forty years. I feel now as if I am still a queen, but a queen without a crown."

I quickly responded to her, "You are the Queen of the Arts, and that crown does not go away. It only grows."

I did not know at the time that she was writing the story of this book, the one that describes the life of a queen in the glory of a royal palace and relinquishing her crown after her divorce. It was the story of a simple unsuspecting teen who was rushed since the age of fifteen into a life she had not known or expected. It was the story of a young, passionate, and impressionable schoolgirl that was infatuated by the glamour of the royal living she was not accustomed to. For no fault of her own, the schoolgirl got embroiled in a high political drama she could not control, but which she had to leave with respect for her own pride and sanity.

Farouk Was My First and Only Love

Queen Farida was able to keep a fine line between her love for King Farouk and her bitterness against the people who corrupted and ruined his life. She had no control over what Farouk did, even though she tried, until she gave up and asked for her divorce. Farouk, not cognizant of what was happening to him or even caring about his future and the future of the country, ended up succumbing to his exile by the Revolutionary Council in 1952. It was the revolution that rose against the palace corruption and a king's life of immorality that the country could not cope with. The people and the country were not getting the leadership needed, especially at that particular time with the Arab–Israeli War that brought down the Arab forces, including the Egyptian forces.

When the revolution took place in 1952, the Revolutionary Council confiscated all of Farida's personal belongings, including her jewelry and everything she had. While she had been divorced for four years before the revolution, she still suffered enormously, as if she was still the queen. She was not bitter for having everything taken from her, except for a box of her personal pictures and the images of her daughters. All the memories of her life at the palace were taken away for no reason. That box, which was of no use to anyone, was in the basement floor of her palace at the Pyramids, where she lived after her divorce from Farouk. The palace too was taken from her.

Farida said, "To me, it was like my life's history recorded in pictures representing each moment of my life with Farouk and my daughters. Taken away, they left me nothing to memorialize that period of my life."

As we sat at the hotel waiting for our meeting with the prince, we were informed that we would be meeting His Highness, Prince Eissa Ibn Salman Al Khalifa, the prince of Bahrain, at ten in the morning on October 20, 1986. When we arrived at the meeting, we were surprised to find the prince and his whole cabinet in attendance, as if it was a business meeting. During the meeting, the prince expressed his great love, admiration, and respect for Egypt and the Egyptian people. His Highness acknowledged the Egyptian's efforts in support of Bahrain's education and cultural developments. He also applauded Egyptian President Mubarak's efforts on behalf of Egypt in the development of Bahrain and the Bahraini people.

Queen Farida responded and talked about her life and her passion for the arts. She described how art, for her, was an important part of her life, even though it was difficult to do, especially if one wanted to be a professional artist. She also talked about the many difficulties Egypt and the Arab countries' had and how they had far-reaching potential, if they worked together and utilized all their combined resources for one and only one goal, the empowerment of their peoples on the world stage.

The discussions continued further when the Bahraini minister of information joined us. Queen Farida continued her comments about the important relations between Bahrain and Egypt and how she wished it would be with all the other Arab countries as well.

The meeting continued in the royal Bahraini palace, where discussion of the subject of Egyptian and Arab cooperation continued. It was important for queen Farida to point out that it was essential for the advancement of all the Arab countries to take their proper places on the world stage.

Our visit to Bahrain continued for more than two weeks, during which the queen's art show received great acclaim. We had many visits from many dignitaries who came, not only to greet the Egyptian queen, but also to admire her work in the arts.

Queen Farida: The Last Chapter, The Noble Farewell

In one of our meetings, Queen Farida told me, "President Mubarak established a monthly pension for me of four hundred Egyptian pounds. He also ordered the purchase of an apartment for me, the one I am living in now. I will not forget Mrs. Suzan Mubarak taking care of me when I was ill, always asking about me and resolving a lot of the bureaucratic difficulties I faced. She really cared for me, and I always appreciated her attention not just to me but also for her constant social and charitable activities.

"The country, represented by President Mubarak and Prime Minister Dr. Atef Sedki, took care of all my medical expenses, which continue until now. The president also provided me with a diplomatic passport, and you know how this was a dream for me." The queen laughed. "I consider myself an Egyptian ambassador without portfolio. You know how much I love Egypt."

I quickly responded, "You are an ambassador and an honorable ambassador for Egypt at that. I witnessed that myself in Paris, London, and Bahrain this last time. I saw how you represented Egypt with great honor everywhere.

The queen smiled. "This is a testament I shall always cherish."

I responded, "All of Egypt, the government and its people, are proud of you and hold you with the greatest admiration and love. They all know the sacrifices you endured and the efforts you made on their behalf at a time you could have just looked the other way."

President Hosni Mubarak and His wife Suzan Mubarak,
who stood behind queen Farida, especially in her
last chapter, with illness and other needs.

That was the last meeting I had with Queen Farida. After which, there were no communications between us. I called her on the phone just before her death.

She said to me, "You know I am not supposed to talk to anyone, but when I knew it was you on the phone, I insisted to talk to you."

She asked me about my family, my wife, Nadia, and my daughters, Amira and Ronda. We ended the phone call to meet again, but her fate came ahead of my having another chance to see her or talk to her. She'll always be in my heart.

She hated sickness and loved life and work. Her work kept her remain strong. It helped her resist, and most often, conquer her illnesses among the many other difficulties she faced throughout her life. When she knew from her doctors about her latest condition, she was shaken up and fell into a state of sadness and depression.

She had just had a medical checkup and did all the necessary laboratory tests that were needed at several hospitals in Cairo. She also had an operation at Dr. Ibrahim Badran's Hospital. Dr. Badran, a well-known and a most experienced doctor, performed the operation and did not charge her any fees. He simply refused to accept any payment from the queen. That is what we all know of Dr. Badran, an incredible man in his own right.

Before her last trip to Europe, she fell ill again, which made her more depressed and very nervous. She went through many additional tests, which the doctors prescribed at the Military Hospital in Maadi. When the results came back, it showed she had leukemia, an illness that required her to go through blood transfusions every six months. She had blood transfusions once in Austria and once more in France before she came back to Egypt.

There it was, Egypt, the country the queen adored throughout her life, giving Farida back a small installment of what was due her, a four hundred-pound monthly pension and an apartment in Maadi. When Mrs. Mubarak learned of the queen's illness, she visited her several times to check on her progress. Mrs. Mubarak also contacted the prime minister and requested that the government pay for the queen's medical expenses, including sending her to Paris for treatment at one of the most reputable cancer centers in France.

After a short medical stay in Paris, Queen Farida came back to Cairo, where she was treated at the Military Hospital in Maadi. She then traveled again to the United States for further treatment, where she was diagnosed as having hepatitis from her blood transfusions. Dr. Yasin Abdel Ghafar last treated Farida for leukemia at the Safa Hospital in Dokky, Cairo.

It was ironic that, at the end of the treatment, a fight ensued between the government and the Safa Hospital. Interestingly enough, the fight was about who was to pay for Queen Farida's treatment expenses. The Safa Hospital did not want to accept payment for their services while the government was insisting to pay. The problem was eventually resolved by splitting the payment, and the hospital accepted only half of the charges.

Queen Farida's last visit to Switzerland followed her treatment at the Safa Hospital. She went to visit her daughters and grandchildren, Fadia, Shamel, and Ali. While in Switzerland, Farida fell ill again and was admitted to the hospital, but without recourse, her health had deteriorated considerably, and death was looming over her. She knew that was her end, as there was no relief from her pain. So she insisted on going back to Cairo.

In Cairo, she was admitted to the intensive care unit at Al Badrawi Nile Hospital in Maadi where she gave her last breath on October 16, 1988, at the age of sixty-eight, a life that included eleven years as the crowned queen of Egypt, followed by a life in solitude before she went back to her ovation in the arts. After a long struggle with health problems, Queen Farida finally succumbed to her eternal life in the hereafter.

Around her noble body, her daughters stood by, giving their final farewell to their mother, with sadness visibly showing on their faces and tears in their eyes. Fadia, the queen's favorite daughter, was quietly crying, while Ferial and Fawzyia held back their tears. Joining in the small ceremony were a few close friends who stood quietly remembering their mother and former queen.

Queen Farida's funeral procession was somber, led by many of the government dignitaries and Egyptians who remembered the days of the monarchy and the queen. Those were the older people who wanted to pay their respect and their own farewell to their former queen, Farida, before her body was laid to rest in the dust of Egypt.

الوداع النبيل جنازة الملكة فريدة ، ويرى وسط الصورة مندوب الرئيس مبارك وفى أقصى اليمين المستشار فاروق هاشم مؤلف الكتاب ثم الأستاذين سعيد وشريف ذو الفقار شقيقا الملكة ثم تأمل وصل ثم الدكتور بفارس خالل ووزير الداخلية والنان فاروق حسني وزير الثقافة ثم الدكتور عبد الأحد، جمال الدين

Queen Farida's Funeral with many official dignitaries leading the procession. Many ordinary Egyptians turned out to show their fondness and respect of their former Queen.

Her will was so much stronger than her frail body. Her fierce resistance was beyond her own energy, and her soul was floating far above, wanting to fly, while her exhausted body lay still in bed. The needle shots delivering medicines into her small veins had weakened her body, and pain was like a quiet earthquake, slowly shutting down her life until one last jolt pushed her soul out to the heavens, where it could go back to its creator, the Almighty God.

Appendices

Appendix I

The Happy Royal Wedding Celebration

The Kobba Palace was dressed since yesterday morning with beautiful chains of flowers and roses intertwined in continuous strings, along with electrically lighted chains decorated with magnificent Arabic artworks all around the palace. And there were those lighted panels with different colors capturing His Royal Highness King Farouk's name.

The police and the royal guard, in their beautiful blue dress, stood by the palace doors and along the palace pathways and hallways. There also stood the royal knights on their horses by the palace doors. Some of the attending guard ushered the invited dignitaries to their places in the palace celebration halls. There was also a contingent of artillery brigade led by Lieutenant General Hussein Hosni Al-Zedi Bek, commander of the artillery brigade, to fire the salutary artilleries at the completion of the royal wedding.

At ten thirty yesterday morning, a royal limousine arrived at the palace, bringing the noble fiancée, and with her was her Royal Highness Princess, Neamat Hashem, the king's aunt, who were met with great cheers from the attending public around the palace, chanting with the king's life.

The Invitees

The invitees and dignitaries began to arrive from ten o'clock. The first arrival was His Royal Highness Prince Mohamed Ali and His Honor Mohamed Mahmoud Pasha. They both sat in the grand hall chatting with each other. Following them came His Highness, the dignitaries, and the cabinet members.

At ten twenty arrived His Honor Mohamed Tawfik Nasim Pasha, and he took his place next to the cabinet ministers. He was followed by His Honor Ahmed Zeur Pasha and shook hands with all present, congratulating everyone saying, "Mabrouk, Mabrouk. God willing, we'll all be happy," as he greeted them one by one.

Then came His Honor Moustafa El-Nahas Pasha, the prime minister, and sat with His Honor Mahmoud Bassiouny, the head of the upper house of Parliament. Then followed His Honor Dr. Ahmed Maher, the leader of the lower house of Parliament; His Honor Abdel Hamid Badrawi Pasha, chief justice and the head of the appellate court; His Honor Sheik Abdel-Moniem Selim and Sheik Fathallah Soliman, the chief justice of the High Sharia Court; and Mr. Mohamed Al-Biblawy, among other dignitaries.

The King

At ten forty-five, the king went to his private office and invited the Grand Sheik-Ul-Azhar and His Honor, the chief justice of the Sharia Court. There also entered the witness to the marriage contract, His Honor Ali Maher Pasha, His Honor Said Zul-Faquar Pasha, and His Honor Youssef Zul-Faquar Pasha, the bride's father and her representative according to the Sharia Law.

The Wedding Proceedings in Accordance with the Islamic Sharia

His Royal Highness sat with Sheik Al Azhar, where his eminence Sheik Al Azhar recited the legal oath of offer and acceptance, customary in Islamic weddings, and the questions regarding the dowry current and promised. After these proceedings were completed, the marriage document was recorded in the official royal notary, making two copies, one that was signed by His Royal Highness and delivered to His Honor Youssef Pasha Zul-Faquar, the representative of the bride. And the other was signed by him and given to His Royal Highness.

The Dignitaries and Government Court Congratulations

Upon completion of the official proceedings of the wedding, the Artillery Brigade fired 101 cannons announcing the completion of the wedding ceremony and officiating the marriage between King Farouk and his queen, Queen Farida Zul-Faquar. After which, the dignitaries offered their congratulations to His Royal Highness and offered their prayers for his life and good health. This was followed by an air show from the air force, parading their planes and performing acrobatic maneuvers for the people in celebration of the wedding. This was followed by the palace personnel giving the invitees gifts and mementos, made up of gold boxes containing candy and other sweets in commemoration of the royal wedding. A special gift was given to Sheik Al Azhar, which was a shawl made of cashmere with his eminence's name embroidered on it. Sheik Al Azhar accepted the gift and offered his prayers for long and happy life for His Royal Highness and his bride.

Royal Medal of the Highest Honor to the Queen

At the end of the formal ceremony, His Royal Highness, with his royal order, bequeathed the highest medal onto the queen, a privilege given only to crowned queens.

The Great Nile Medal Bestowed onto the Queen's Father

Then His Royal Highness ordered a royal proclamation onto the queen's father, His Honor Youssef Zul-Faquar, the highest medal of the Great Nile, who gratefully accepted the offered medal.

Appendix II

The February 4, 1942, British Troops Encirclement of the Abdeen Royal Palace

Several reports by the Royal Palace Guard included the official reports by the Royal Palace Guard, declaring and describing the impending attack by the British troops and tanks that had circled the Abdeen Palace. These reports described in great detail the number of tanks and their armaments, along with a detailed description of the troops that had gathered around the palace in an attack mode.

Appendix III

The July 1952 Revolution Declaration

From the Chief of Staff of the Armed Forces to the Egyptian People:

Egypt has been through difficult times in its recent history, plagued with corruption, debauchery and instability in its governance. It is because of these many factors which had an enormous impact on the Armed Forces; and where this corruption and its forces, caused our defeat in Palestine; and since after the war, the forces of corruption banned together against the Armed Forces, appointing corrupt, incompetent and traitors to the Army leadership, so that Egypt would become without an Army that can protect her.

Therefore, we have cleaned-up our ranks and insured that our armed forces are lead by honorable, competent, honest and national leaders, whom we trust, and with their capabilities with the People behind them; we are certain that the Egyptian People shall receive these news with the greatest acceptance and happiness. And that those whom we arrested from the former army officers, shall not be harmed and will be released at the appropriate time.

And I assure the Egyptian People that the Army with all of its ranks are now working in the best interest of the Country under the constitution with no hidden agenda or ulterior motives.

I take this opportunity to ask the Egyptian People to not allow any of the traitors to resort to violence or any destructive actions, as this is not in the best interest of Egypt. Any such action will be met with the utmost force that has not been seen before and that the perpetrators shall immediately receive the punishment of treason. The army shall proceed with its duties in cooperation with the Police forces. I would like to re-assure our brothers the foreigners in Egypt, that their well-being, their wealth; their jobs and their families shall be safe and that the Armed forces shall be committed to their protection. With God, the overseer of our actions.

ملحق رقم « ٣ »

بيـــان ثـورة يوليـــو سنة ١٩٥٢

من القائد العام للقوات المسلحة الى الشعب المصرى

اجتازت مصر فترة عصيبة في تاريخها الأخير من الرشوة والفساد وعدم استقرار الحكم . وقد كان لكل هذه العوامل تأثير كبير على الجيش وبسبب الرشوة المفروضة في ضربتنا في حرب فلسطين وإما فترة ما بعد لهذه الحرب فقد تضافرت فيها عوامل الفساد وتآمر الخونة على الجيش وتولى أمره إما جاهل او خائن او فاسد حتى تصبح مصر بلا جيش يحميها ، وعلى ذلك فقد قمنا بتطهير أنفسنا وتولى امرنا في داخل الجيش رجال نثق في قدرتهم وفي خلقهم وفي وطنيتهم ولابد أن مصر ستستقبل هذا النصر بالابتهاج والترحيب

اما من رأينا اعتقالهم من رجال الجيش السابقين فهؤلاء لن ينالهم ضرر وسيطلق سراحهم في الوقت المناسب

وانى اؤكد للشعب المصرى ان الجيش اليوم كله اصبح يعمل لصالح الوطن في ظل الدستور مجردا من أية غاية .

وانتهز لهذه الفرصة فأطلب من الشعب الا يسمح لأحد من الخونة بأن يلجأ لأعمال التخريب او العنف لأن هذا ليس في صالح مصر وإنه اي عمل من هذا القبيل سيقابل بشدة لم يسبق لها مثيل وسيلقى فاعله جزاء الخائن والخال وسيقوم الجيش بواجبه هذا متعاونا مع البوليس وانى اطمئن اخواننا الاجانب على مصالحهم وأعراضهم وأموالهم ويعتبر الجيش نفسه مسئولا عنهم والله ولى التوفيق «

« إنـــذار محمـــد نجيــب إلى المـلك فـــاروق »

« من الفريق أركان حرب محمد نجيب .. باسم ضباط الجيش ورجاله إلى جلالة الملك فاروق الأول :

« إنه نظرا لما لاقته البلاد في العهد الأخير من فوضى شاملة عمت جميع المرافق نتيجة سوء تصرفكم وعبثكم بالدستور وامتهانكم لإرادة الشعب حتى أصبح كل فرد من أفراده لا يطمئن على حياته وماله أو كرامته ولقد ساءت سمعة مصر بين شعوب العالم من تماديكم في هذا المسلك حتى أصبح الخونة والمرتشون يجدون في ظلكم الحماية والأمن والثراء الفاحش والإسراف الماجن على حساب الشعب الجائع الفقير ولقد تجلت أية ذلك في حرب فلسطين وما تبعها من فضائح الأسلحة الفاسدة وما ترتب عليها من محاكمات تعرضت لتدخلكم السافر مما أفسد الحقائق وزعزع الثقة في العدالة وساعد الخونة على رسم هذه الخطى فأثرى من أثرى ، وفجر من فجر ، وكيف لا والناس على دين ملوكهم ، لذلك قد فوضني الجيش الممثل لقوة الشعب أن أطلب من جلالتكم التنازل عن العرش لسمو ولي عهدكم الأمير أحمد فؤاد على أن يتم ذلك في موعد غايته الساعة الثانية عشرة من ظهر اليوم (السبت الموافق ٢٦ من يوليو ١٩٥٢ والرابع من ذي القعدة سنة ١٣٧١) . ومغادرة البلاد قبل الساعة السادسة من مساء اليوم نفسه . والجيش يحمل جلالتكم كل ما يترتب على عدم النزول على رغبة الشعب من نتائج » .

الإسكندرية في يوم السبت   توقيع
٤ من ذي القعدة ١٣٧١ هـ   محمد نجيب
(٢٦ يوليو سنة ١٩٥٢ ميلادية)   فريق أركان حرب

* * * * *

وكان من رأي جمال سالم إعدام فاروق وإلا يسمح له بمغادرة البلاد ، أو يصطحب معه أية ممتلكات ، ولكن نجيب لم يوافق .. ومن ثم ترك الأمر لمجلس القيادة في القاهرة كـ ست في الأم ..

A copy of the actual declarations and ultimatum from
the Officers Revolutionary Council to King Farouk and
the Egyptian People on the 26th of July, 1952.,

Mohamed Naguib's Ultimatum to King Farouk

Addendum #3

From Field Marshal Mohamed Naguib:

In the name of the Army officers and its men, to His Royal Highness King Farouk the First:

It is due to what the country has suffered recently of complete chaos that has taken over the country's institutions, which was the result of your mismanagement of the country's affairs, your toying with the constitution and disrespect for the people's good will, such that every member of the society can no longer feel secure for his life, his financial well being or his honor; that Egypt's reputation and respect amongst its people and the peoples of the world as a result of your continuing this path which has opened the door for the corrupts and the traitors among your associate, to accumulate enormous wealth and be protected by you, all at the expense of the poor and hungry among the Egyptian people. It has become abundantly clear, especially during the war in Palestine, and what followed from scandals about your arrogant interference in the proceeding of the trials in the courts about the faulty weapons, which brought mistrust in the judicial system and helped those traitors plan what they wanted accumulating more and more wealth. And why not, people will follow and take the lead from their rulers and overseers in as mush as they are allowed.

Therefore, I have been delegated by the Armed Forces, the Representative of the People's power, to ask your Royal Highness to relinquish the Throne to his Royal Highness, your heir, Prince Ahmed Fouad, and that this is completed at a time no later than Twelve O'clock, "Noon" today, Saturday the 26th of July 1952, the

Fourth of Thee-ElQui3da, 1371 of the Islamic Calendar; and to leave the Country before Six O'clock in the evening of the same day. The Army holds your Royal Highness responsible for all the Consequences of not acquiescing to the People's wishes.

Signed,

Mohamed Naguib

Field marshal.

Alexandria,

Saturday, 4 Thee—El Qui3da, 1371

The 26th of July, 1952

Appendix IV

Royal Decree Number 65 for the Year 1952

We, Farouk The First, King of Egypt and Sudan,

Since we have always wanted what is best for our People and wished them happiness and prosperity; and since we want, in the most sincere way, to hold the country harmless from all the difficulties that she faces at these sensitive and difficult times, and in response to the People wishes,

We have therefore decided to relinquish our Throne to our heir, Prince Ahmed Fouad and have passed our order to the Honorable, Ali Maher Pasha, the Prime Minister for its execution.

Produced at Raas El-Tien Palace on the 4th of Thee El-Qu3ida, 1371. (The 26th of July, 1952).

Signed,

Farouk the First

أمر ملكى رقم ٦٥ لسنة ١٩٥٢

نحن فاروق الأول ملك مصر والسودان

لما كنا نطلب الخير وإنما لأنفسنا وتبتغي سعادتنا وربها
ولما كنا نرغب رغبة أكيدة فى تجنيب البلاد المصاعب التى تواجهها فى هذه الظروف الدقيقة
ونزولا على إرادة الشعب

فقد نزلنا عن العرش لولي عهدنا الأمير أحمد فؤاد وأسندنا أمر بلادنا إلى حضرة صاحب
المقام الرفيع على ماهر باشا رئيس مجلس الوزراء للعمل بمقتضاه
صدر بقصر رأس التين فى ذى الحجة ١٣٧١ (٢٦ يوليو ١٩٥٢).

نهاية ملك .. أو « الأمر الملكى » بتنازل الملك الذى
غدر بنفسه .. وبشعبه .. قبل ان يغدر به اى احد !!

King Farouk's acquiescence to the Ultimatum and
relinquishing the throne to his son Ahmed Fouad.

Appendix V

Constitutional Declaration from the Leadership of the Revolutionary Council

In the name of God, "the most Gracious most Merciful"

Since the Revolution, from its beginning, was aiming at ending the colonial occupation and its supporters; it demanded, on the 26th of July 1952, the former King Farouk to relinquish his "Throne", since he was the corner stone from which the occupation derived its powers.

Since that time and since the dissolution of the Political Parties, some people found their opportunity and their protection from the extension of the powers of the Royal regime, after the overthrow of the King. Therefore, the People have demanded the total elimination of these people from the society.

And since, the history of the Mohamed Ali dynasty in Egypt was a continuous series of treasons that were committed against the people, the first of which was Ismail's irresponsible behavior and excessive expenditures on his pleasures, a matter that put the country in enormous debits which in turn put the Country's finances in trouble and ruined its reputation providing the occupying powers a leverage which they can use for their influence in this peaceful Country.

Then came Tawfik who continued and completed this blatant treason to hold on to his throne giving the opportunity to the occupying forces to enter the country to protect the foreigner on the Throne, who sought the help of the enemy against his own people. With that, the occupying enemy and the king on the throne, became one and the same, each protecting the other against the people. And so, each used the other's influence to repress the people and exhaust the country's resources, destroying, in the process, the people's will, self esteem and their freedom.

Farouk far exceeded all of his predecessors in that family tree, so he accumulated more wealth, and lived the life of corruption and disrepute, bringing his own end and fate. So it is time for the country to free itself from all this slavery that the people were exposed to.

Therefore and because of all what the people and the country has been through;

We declare, in the name of the people:

First: The dissolution of the Monarchy System; and the end to the rule of the Mohamed Ali Family; and the cancellation of all the titles of the members of this family.

Second: Proclaim the Republic, with the President; General Mohamed Naguib, the leader of the revolution, as the President of the Republic, while keeping all of his current authority under the temporary constitution.

Third: This system shall continue during the transitional period and the people shall have the last word in determining the nature of the republic and choose the President when the New Constitution is established (Approved).

Therefore, we must have trust and faith in God and ourselves and be proud of God's choosing from amongst his believers.

Cairo, 7th of Shawal, 1372

18th of June, 1953.

Signed:

Army Chief of Staff

General Mohamed Nageib

Colonel Gamal Abdel Nasser

Colonel Abdel-Latif Baghdadi

Colonel Anwar El Sadat

Major Abdel Hakim Amer

Major Kamal El-Din Hussein

Colonel Gamal Salem

Colonel Hussein Ibrahim

Colonel Salah Salem

Colonel Hussein El Shafie

Major Khaled Mohy El-Din

Colonel Zakaria Mohy El Din

إعلان دستوري
من مجلس قيادة الثورة

بسم الله الرحمن الرحيم

صورة البيان الدستوري الذي أصدرته ثورة ٢٣ يوليو بإسقاط النظام الملكي وإعلان نظام الجمهورية في مصر .. وعليه توقيعات أعضاء مجلس قيادة الثورة . بتقدمها توقيع اللواء محمد نجيب رئيس مجلس القيادة.

A copy of the constitutional declaration by the Revolutionary Council ending the Monarchy system of government in Egypt, ending the Mohamed Ali dynasty's rule of Egypt, and changing the system of government to a Republic. Declaration was signed by the Revolutionary Council officers. N

Printed in Great Britain
by Amazon